"Fascinating. Here is a thought-provoking book that will guide teens and adults to a deeper understanding of our country and its laws. Superior."
—*KLIATT*

"Excellent." —*Booklist*

A "Quick Pick" nominee
—American Library Association / YALSA

Teens Take It to Court

Young People Who Challenged the Law—and Changed Your Life

Judge Tom Jacobs

free spirit
PUBLiSHiNG®

Helping kids
help themselves™
since 1983

Library of Congress Cataloging-in-Publication Data
Jacobs, Thomas A.
    Teens take it to court : young people who challenged the law—and changed your life / by Thomas A. Jacobs.
        p. cm.
    Includes bibliographical references and index.
    ISBN-13: 978-1-57542-199-5
    ISBN-10: 1-57542-199-2
    1. Teenagers—Legal status, laws, etc.—United States—Juvenile literature. 2. Teenagers—Civil rights—United States—Juvenile literature. 3. Parent and child (Law)—United States—Juvenile literature. 4. Actions and defenses—United States—Juvenile literature. I. Title.
KF479.Z9J329 2006
349.73083'5--dc22

                                                                    2005033141

At the time of this book's publication, all facts and figures cited are the most current available. All telephone numbers, addresses, and Web site URLs are accurate and active; all publications, organizations, Web sites, and other resources exist as described in this book; and all have been verified as of January 2006. The author and Free Spirit Publishing make no warranty or guarantee concerning the information and materials given out by organizations or content found at Web sites, and we are not responsible for any changes that occur after this book's publication. If you find an error or believe that a resource listed here is not as described, please contact Free Spirit Publishing. Parents, teachers, and other adults: We strongly urge you to monitor children's use of the Internet.

Edited by Catherine Broberg and Elizabeth Verdick
Cover and interior design by Marieka Heinlen

10 9 8 7 6 5 4 3 2 1

Free Spirit Publishing Inc.
217 Fifth Avenue North, Suite 200
Minneapolis, MN 55401-1299
(612) 338-2068
help4kids@freespirit.com
www.freespirit.com

Free Spirit Publishing is a member of the Green Press Initiative, and we're committed to printing our books on recycled paper containing a minimum of 30% post-consumer waste (PCW). For every ton of books printed on 30% PCW recycled paper, we save 5.1 trees, 2,100 gallons of water, 114 gallons of oil, 18 pounds of air pollution, 1,230 kilowatt hours of energy, and .9 cubic yards of landfill space. At Free Spirit it's our goal to nurture not only young people, but nature too!

Dedication

This book is dedicated to our nation's teenagers—those profiled in this book who have already made a difference, and those willing to take a stand on issues of freedom and individual rights. It is also dedicated to the next generation of teens, including Parker, Chase, Austin, Taylor, Kali, Pauly, Cody, Netaya, Kylie, Alexandra, Sandy, MacKenzie Kate, and Shelby.

Acknowledgments

One of the challenges of writing this book was locating the people involved in the cases. Thanks to all who helped in the effort and particularly to those who granted me interviews. Your willingness to discuss the issues in your case was an invaluable contribution to this project.

Thanks also to Judy Galbraith, and her great staff at Free Spirit Publishing, for the opportunity to write and revise this book. The experience, guidance, and wisdom of editors Cathy Broberg and Elizabeth Verdick are appreciated beyond these few words. Appreciation is also extended to Judge Maurice Portley and Judge Emmet J. Ronan, who somehow found time to review the manuscript, and to Justice Ruth Bader Ginsburg for her words of inspiration on the cover. In the spirit of saving the best for last, I must also acknowledge my judicial assistant, Jami Taylor. Without her skills, personality, and patience, life at court would have been very trying.

Contents

Foreword

"Children have a very special place in life which law should reflect."
—Mr. Justice Frankfurter, concurring in *May v. Anderson*, 345 U.S. 528, 536 (1953)

The United States of America has the finest legal system in the world. Created at the time our nation was born, our courts and laws have undergone much change over the past 230 years. Judge Tom Jacobs's book, *Teens Take It to Court*, chronicles how the American legal system has attempted to reflect the "special place" that children have in our society. His book has something for everyone.

First, it is a civics lesson. The cases describe the process we, as a society, have followed to establish rules and guidelines for how we deal with our children. Many of them reflect the ongoing philosophical debate that began in 1776 about our rights as individual citizens and the power of our government. A parent's right to set rules for his or her child versus the child's right to make individual choices and the authority of school officials to maintain order versus the individual rights of students are just two examples where courts are constantly trying to find the proper balance between equally valid, but often conflicting, interests.

Readers will also feel like they are in law school. Roscoe Pound said that "The law must be stable, but it must not stand still." As you read this fascinating book, you will see how courts have tried to establish stability by providing guidance for schools, parents, children, and others for future cases. However, you will also learn how difficult it is to establish "bright line" rules that will fit all cases, and that court cases on similar issues often differ depending on the facts or society's evolution.

1

Finally, this is a collection of short stories of individual courage and perseverance by young people and parents. Many of these cases were brought into the legal system by parents or guardians on behalf of children. Together they stood up for something they believed in through countless court hearings that often spanned years. Their commitment to principles and ideas that were important to them has had a profound influence on the lives of children and families in this country.

Teens Take It to Court will remind you of the many challenges we have faced as the country has grown and matured. It will educate you about the current state of the law. Hopefully it will challenge you to think about, and become active in, the issues that children, families, and society are dealing with in the new millennium.

Emmet J. Ronan
Presiding Judge, Maricopa County Juvenile Court
Mesa, Arizona

Introduction

Do you remember the first time somebody told you that life isn't fair? Maybe you were shocked and didn't want to accept it as true. Fairness, after all, is something we've been taught to work for in life. Parents strive to treat all of their children equally, to not give one more than another. Schools promote the idea of fairness, to provide every student with an opportunity to succeed. And we learn that we should treat other people as we want to be treated ourselves—in other words, to be fair. So when we learn that life isn't fair, either through words or personal experiences, we're often very disappointed.

The good news is that our country's judicial system is designed to provide "justice for all." Justice means following the laws, setting things right, or correcting a wrong.

As a juvenile court judge for twenty years, I had the honor of working with thousands of teenagers and their families to bring about justice. Courts are called on to answer questions and resolve problems about all aspects of life, including crime, individual rights, and relationships at home, work, and school. This means going to court isn't limited to kids who get into trouble. Young people also come into the courtroom to challenge rules in their school, to file claims of sexual harassment, to participate in custody hearings, and more.

Through my experience with families in the court system, I've learned that many people think this part of the government is mysterious and confusing. That's unfortunate, because the law is for you—*the people*—and isn't the exclusive property of lawyers and judges.

Looking at cases brought before the U.S. Supreme Court is a good way to learn more about the law and the judicial system. And because the Court hears cases involving our constitutional rights, its decisions affect everyone—including you.

> When you understand how the courts work, you have the knowledge that can help you achieve fairness in your own life and in the lives of others.

This book is divided into two parts. Part 1 contains answers to questions you may have about the U.S. Supreme Court and the U.S. Constitution. Whether this information is new to you or you read it as a refresher, it will help you understand the significance of the cases that follow. Part 2 presents twenty-one cases about teenagers and a few children who were involved in important court cases. Most of the cases were reviewed by the U.S. Supreme Court. In some cases, the teens challenge a law they don't agree with; other cases focus on the rights of teens and children charged with a crime; and still other cases concern the protections young people have under the law.

You may notice the following about some of the U.S. Supreme Court cases and the related cases in this book: (1) some include more details than others, (2) some use the full names of the participants, while others contain abbreviated

> Not all of the teens featured in this book are role models. In fact, some committed crimes. Yet, the results of all the cases affect the rights and responsibilities that all American teens have today.

names, and (3) the final decisions in several cases aren't given. This is because each state has different confidentiality laws (laws that restrict how much juvenile court information is made public). For example, some states require that only a juvenile's initials be used, while other states allow the first name and the initial of the last name. Also, when cases before an appeals court are sent back to the lower court, the final results sometimes aren't made public.

The cases you read may spur further questions in your mind. If you want to learn more about the cases and why they were decided a certain way, check out the section in Part 1 called "How to Do Legal Research." You'll find lots of tips for doing in-depth research on the decisions of the U.S. Supreme Court.

In reviewing the cases contained in this book, you'll come across certain legal terms that may be new to you. Terms in **bold** are included in the glossary at the end of the book (see pages 192–197). Other terms are explained within the cases. However, the legalese, or legal language, is kept to a minimum. This is consistent with today's legal profession, which is attempting to speak more English and less Latin.

> As you read these cases, you'll discover that the law is flexible; it sometimes has to change to meet the needs of a nation that's constantly changing and growing. However, you'll also see that the common thread is fairness, in the proceedings and to the participants.

Teens Take It to Court allows you to participate in the U.S. Supreme Court cases under discussion. Each case begins with an outline of the facts—this is the information that a judge or jury would hear. Next, you're given a set of questions to help you consider the issues. (You can think about how you'd decide the case.) The ruling, or decision, is then revealed, including the Court's reasoning. Related cases, which illustrate the ongoing debate over these issues in courtrooms across the nation, are presented next. In a few cases in the book, the issues remain unsettled, with U.S. Supreme Court decisions yet to come. At the end of each case, you'll find discussion-starters or activities to help you get more involved in the issues that interest you.

I'm always interested in hearing from teens about their experiences and questions. If you'd like to get in touch with me, you can contact me in care of:

Free Spirit Publishing
217 Fifth Avenue North, Suite 200
Minneapolis, MN 55401-1299

Or email me at: help4kids@freespirit.com

I look forward to hearing from you!

Tom Jacobs, J.D.

Part 1:
Understanding the Law

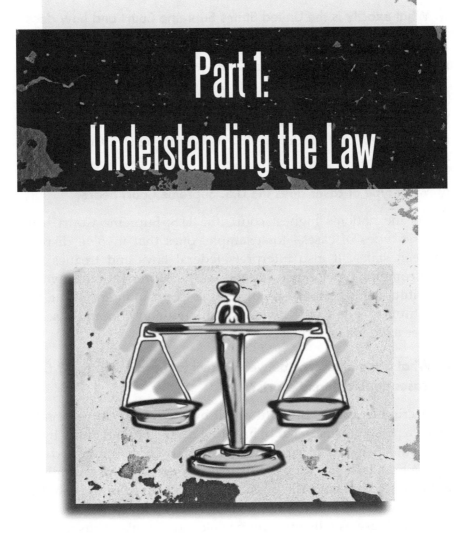

The Supreme Court and How It Works

Q. **What exactly is the United States Supreme Court and how does it differ from other courts in our country?**

A. The United States Supreme Court was created by federal law in 1789. It's the highest court in the nation, and its decisions affect all of our lives. The Court's job is to settle lawsuits and interpret the U.S. Constitution. It has the final say in cases brought before it. (For more on the Constitution, see "Facts About the U.S. Constitution" on pages 16–19.)

Q. **What type of cases does the U.S. Supreme Court hear?**

A. As the nation's highest court, the U.S. Supreme Court hears specific types of cases—for example, ones that involve disputes between states. It also interprets federal laws and treaties. The most common type of case before the U.S. Supreme Court involves constitutional questions—requiring the Court to interpret the U.S. Constitution. The Court reviews both civil and criminal cases, as long as a federal issue exists.

Q. **What is the difference between a civil and a criminal case? Do the cases go to different courts?**

A. A criminal case is brought about by a government prosecutor, when a person is suspected of breaking a law. If found guilty by the court, this person receives punishment. The crime committed may be against a local law (city, municipality, or county, for example) or a state or federal law. The possible penalties range from **probation,** to community service or fines, to jail or prison time.

A civil case usually involves private individuals or businesses— one person or group sues another. In this type of case, the verdict may result in a loss of property or money, but not freedom—no one found guilty goes to jail or prison.

In larger cities, criminal and civil cases are tried by separate courts, where the judges specialize in either criminal or civil proceedings. In smaller locales, judges may hear both civil and criminal cases.

Q. How many different types of courts are there?

A. There are two main judicial systems—state and federal. State courts are responsible for settling disputes among their residents. These courts also interpret their state's constitution, as well as state and local laws. In the federal judicial system, the courts preside over lawsuits based on federal laws and the U.S. Constitution. Each judicial system has three levels of courts—one trial court level and two appellate court levels.

Every court has what's called **jurisdiction,** or the responsibility to hear specific types of cases in a certain geographical area. This means that your lawsuit must be filed in the right county or district court. The money at stake in the case also dictates where it may be filed. In other words, a $500 lawsuit may belong in one court, but a $1 million lawsuit belongs in another.

Within the state court system are other courts with specific functions. These include justice courts, police courts, municipal courts, or city courts. Sometimes referred to as lower courts, or courts of limited jurisdiction, they generally handle lesser offenses (**misdemeanors, petty offenses,** and civil cases under a specified dollar amount).

Q. How does the juvenile justice system fit into the justice system as a whole?

A. The juvenile justice system is one of several components of America's justice system. State courts have jurisdiction over civil and criminal cases, as well as the more specialized areas of probate, mental health, domestic relations, tax, and juvenile matters.

Cases handled in the juvenile justice system include **delinquency** matters, dependent children (abused, abandoned, and neglected children), termination of parental rights, and adoption. Sometimes an individual or a family may be involved with several divisions of the court at the same time. For example, a child in a foster home may break the law and end up on probation. At the same time, his or her parents may be in domestic relations court for divorce, custody, or visitation.

Q. What happens in a trial court?

A. In trial courts, juries and judges decide the cases. Most of the court news you hear and read about comes from trials. That's because this is where the excitement and drama of courtroom battles occur. At a trial, the evidence in the case is presented—through witnesses testifying or by use of physical evidence (such as weapons, X-rays, or charts). Either the judge or jury will decide the case, following the presentation of all of the evidence and the closing statements of the attorneys.

Q. What happens in an appellate court?

A. Depending on the type of case, the losing party in trial court may have a right to **appeal.** This means that if you lose your case, you may ask a higher court (an appellate court) to review what happened in the trial. Basically, you're asking for a different decision because of some error made during the trial.

Local rules of court govern whether an appeal is available and to which appellate court it may go. In some jurisdictions, for example, traffic cases may proceed only one level up on an appeal, and go no further. Consequently, your state's highest court may never see a traffic appeal. Most states have two levels of appellate courts, due to the volume of cases. Certain cases are heard by the first level of the court of appeals, with the more significant issues going to the highest state court. These generally review **felony** cases or constitutional issues—which affect all residents of the state.

A case that has gone up to an appellate court is "on appeal." The appellate court doesn't consider new evidence. No witnesses are called to testify, and no jury is involved. Rather, the attorneys make their arguments to the court in writing, called a **brief.** (The lawyers may be allowed to present oral arguments if the court thinks this would be useful in deciding the issues.)

The U.S. Supreme Court is the highest appellate court.

Q. How are cases sent to an appellate court decided? How does this differ from a trial court?

A. The appellate court decides the case by issuing a written statement called an opinion. The cases discussed in this book are the opinions of the state supreme courts and the U.S. Supreme Court. The appellate court may do a number of things in deciding a case. It may reverse the decision of the trial court and send the case back for a new trial. It may also affirm the trial court's decision or modify the decision, as it sees fit.

Q. Why do courts rule differently on the same law?

A. It's important to keep in mind that courts consist of people—and people often have differing opinions. One judge or a panel of judges may be involved. The job of a judge is to consider both the facts of the case and the applicable law. Judges often disagree on the interpretation of a law, however. Consequently, appellate courts may review and decide the issue. If the issue raises what is called a federal question regarding the U.S. Constitution or Bill of Rights, the U.S. Supreme Court may decide the case with a ruling that applies to all jurisdictions.

Q. Who determines whether a judge or a jury will decide a case? What factors are involved in this decision?

A. State and federal laws dictate whether you may request a jury trial. In civil cases, the dollar amount of the case may determine whether a jury trial is allowed. For example, if somebody sues for an amount under $5,000, the case may be tried before a judge, without a jury (sometimes called a bench trial). In criminal cases, the maximum jail sentence may determine whether a jury is allowed. Generally, if the maximum sentence is less than six months in jail, a jury trial isn't available.

Q. How does a case get to the U.S. Supreme Court?

A. The U.S. Constitution gives the U.S. Supreme Court the authority to hear cases. This authority is referred to as the Court's jurisdiction. The cases before the Court fall under two categories—original jurisdiction and appellate jurisdiction.

Original jurisdiction includes cases that go directly to the U.S. Supreme Court, bypassing all other courts. This includes: (1) disputes between states—about boundaries, for example, (2) arguments between the federal government and a state, (3) quarrels among citizens of different states. Cases involving ambassadors to other countries also go directly to the U.S. Supreme Court.

The majority of cases filed with the U.S. Supreme Court each year actually fall under appellate jurisdiction. These are cases from lower federal courts and state courts where a federal law or the Constitution is involved. A case that's handled in a state trial court proceeds up through the state's court of appeals. Most cases stop at the state's highest court, with that decision being final. However, if there's a federal issue in the case involving a constitutional right, the case may then go to the federal courts for resolution. For example, if the case involves freedom of speech and you lose in the state courts, you may file a **petition** asking the U.S. Supreme Court to review the case. This is because the First Amendment to the Constitution guarantees speech as a protected right. (See the **Bill of Rights** on pages 18–19.)

As you'll see in Part 2, it may take three to five years for a case to make its way through the state and federal systems and then, if accepted for review by the U.S. Supreme Court, to obtain a final decision.

Q. Who's responsible for seeing that a case gets to the U.S. Supreme Court? The individuals involved or their attorneys?

A. A case that's appealed to a higher court involves writing and arguing about legal issues. The litigants (parties to the lawsuit), including the juveniles and parents, decide with the advice of their attorney whether to appeal a case. But once the decision is made to pursue an appeal through the legal system, the attorneys are responsible for seeing that all of the rules of court are met. The parties in the case take a backseat and let the lawyers handle the appeal.

Q. Who pays the legal fees in U.S. Supreme Court cases, especially if they take years to be resolved?

A. In criminal cases, the public defender's office usually pays expenses, or in the rare case, a private lawyer does. In civil cases, either the family retains a lawyer or the American Civil Liberties Union (ACLU) becomes involved and pays the cost. (The ACLU is a national organization devoted to protecting the basic rights set forth in the U.S. Constitution.) Occasionally, a private lawyer may take a civil case on *pro bono*—at no fee and as a service to the community—for the principle of the case or to gain exposure for his or her practice.

Q. How does the U.S. Supreme Court decide the cases? What facts or laws are taken into consideration?

A. The full Court is made up of nine justices, or judges, who meet to consider the cases filed each year. They vote on which ones will be granted a full hearing. Oral arguments are scheduled, and both sides submit written arguments, or briefs. One attorney for each side is allowed to argue the case before the justices. Following the arguments, all nine justices meet in total privacy to discuss the case and take a vote. A justice representing the majority is assigned to write the Court's opinion. The other justices may join in the opinion or write their own, agreeing (**concurring**) or disagreeing (**dissenting**).

Q. How are the justices of the U.S. Supreme Court chosen?

A. The U.S. Supreme Court justices are nominated by the President of the United States and must be approved by the U.S. Senate. A justice may remain on the Court for life. Justices don't have to run for re-election and may retire when they wish. One of the justices acts as the Chief Justice of the Court.

Q. How is the Chief Justice chosen?

A. The Chief Justice is nominated by the President of the United States and approved by the U.S. Senate. There's no limit to this person's term; the U.S. Constitution says that the Chief Justice may serve "during good behavior."

In 2005 President George W. Bush nominated John G. Roberts Jr., a judge on a lower court, to replace Chief Justice William H. Rehnquist, who passed away on September 3, 2005. Justice Rehnquist was eighty years old and served thirty-three years on the Court, the last nineteen as Chief Justice. The U.S. Senate voted in favor of the appointment and Judge Roberts became Chief Justice Roberts on September 29, 2005. A new Supreme Court era has begun.

Q. What responsibilities and authority does the Chief Justice of the U.S. Supreme Court have?

A. In addition to presiding over the U.S. Supreme Court and participating in cases before the Court, the Chief Justice has a number of other duties. He or she is head of the federal judiciary, including the Circuit Courts of Appeal and district courts (at least one in each state). The Chief Justice also presides over the U.S. Senate during an impeachment trial of a sitting president. (This happened in 1999, when President William Clinton was impeached by the House of Representatives.) The Chief Justice is also third in line to the president and vice president regarding protocol in receiving visiting dignitaries and ambassadors.

Q. How many cases does the U.S. Supreme Court hear each year?

A. The Court receives more than 7,000 petitions for review each year. It alone has the authority to decide which cases it will hear. In a given year, the Court accepts, hears, and decides approximately 100 cases.

Q. Does a ruling need to be unanimous?

A. The Court's decision doesn't need to be unanimous—the majority vote carries the day. However, the members of the Court who share the minority vote may express their views in **dissenting opinions.** A number of the cases presented in this book were decided by five to four votes, where one vote in the other direction would have made a difference in our lives.

Q. Do U.S. Supreme Court decisions become laws?

A. A decision of the U.S. Supreme Court becomes the authority in the country regarding the specific issue addressed. It's not, however, a law in the same sense as a law passed by a state legislature, or by a city or town. Instead it's an *interpretation* of the Constitution and has the same *effect* as a law. In later cases that raise the same issue, the earlier decision may govern. This is called a precedent, which prevents the same issue from being decided over and over, or differently in different courts. If it can be shown that the earlier decision was in error, it may be set aside or overruled.

Q. When is the Court in session?

A. The U.S. Supreme Court's annual term begins on the first Monday of each October. A summer recess begins in late June.

Q. Where is the U.S. Supreme Court located? Can anyone visit and watch the Court?

A. The U.S. Supreme Court is located in Washington, D.C., at 1 First Street S.E. It's open year-round, Monday through Friday from 9 a.m. to 4:30 p.m. Tours and lectures are available when the Court isn't in session.

Oral arguments are scheduled each year from October to May. They begin at 10 a.m. and are open to the public. Seating for the public is limited and on a first-come, first-seated basis.

For further information on the Court and its justices, check out the following resources:

- The U.S. Supreme Court's public information office: (202) 479-3211

- The U.S. Supreme Court's Web site: *www.supremecourtus.gov*

- The FindLaw Web site: *www.findlaw.com*

- U.S. Supreme Court Multimedia Database: *www.oyez.org*

Facts About the U.S. Constitution

Q. **Who wrote the Constitution? At what point in our country's history did it come about?**

A. After the first thirteen states won their independence from England in 1783, a convention met in Philadelphia in 1787 to draft a plan for the government. It was intended to define the powers of the national government and establish protection for the rights of the states and each of its citizens.

Following four months of discussion and debate, the Constitution was signed on September 17, 1787, at Independence Hall in Philadelphia. There were fifty-five state delegates at the convention who contributed to the content of the Constitution. Among the delegates were George Washington, Benjamin Franklin, Alexander Hamilton, and James Madison, who received the title Father of the Constitution because of his leadership and participation at the convention.

Q. **How and where does the Constitution fit into the structure of our government?**

A. The U.S. Constitution defines the rights and liberties of the American people and establishes a national government. Federal and state judges apply the Constitution in many court cases. The U.S. Supreme Court has the final authority in explaining and interpreting the meaning of the Constitution. It has the power of judicial review, which means that it may declare a law as unconstitutional.

Q. **Why is this document so important?**

A. Our country is based on laws. The U.S. Constitution has been described as a "living" document, even though it was written more than 200 years ago. This is because the Constitution continues to be debated in classrooms and courtrooms across the nation.

Q. Why is it still debated today if it's more than 200 years old? So much has changed since it was written, how can it still be relevant today?

A. The delegates to the Constitutional Convention were writing for the nation's future. They recognized the need for a document that would expand and develop as the United States grew. James Madison said, "In framing a system which we wish to last for ages, we should not lose sight of the changes which ages will produce."

Americans in the 1780s weren't concerned about drugs at school, student protests, abortion rights, or due process for minors. Yet, the Constitution has grown to now address these and other issues that face Americans today.

Q. Which courts debate what the Constitution means? Only the U.S. Supreme Court?

A. Both state and federal courts often face constitutional issues. A court's decision in a case may be based on its interpretation of the U.S. Constitution, and if one of the parties in the lawsuit disagrees with the court's ruling, an appeal may be made. Depending on the nature of the case and its constitutional issue, the U.S. Supreme Court may hear the case and make the final decision.

Q. What about the Bill of Rights and other amendments? How and why did these come into being?

A. During the American Revolution (1775–1783), the states adopted their own constitutions, which guaranteed individual rights of the people. Following the Constitutional Convention in 1787, ten amendments, or additions, to the Constitution were written; by 1791, they were ratified (approved) by the states. These became known as the Bill of Rights. A total of twenty-seven amendments have been passed since 1791.

Bill of Rights—Amendments I to X

I   Congress shall make no law respecting an establishment of religion, or prohibiting the free exercise thereof; or abridging the freedom of speech, or of the press; or the right of the people peaceably to assemble, and to petition the Government for a redress of grievances.

II A well regulated Militia, being necessary to the security of a free State, the right of the people to keep and bear Arms, shall not be infringed.

III No soldier shall, in time of peace be quartered in any house, without the consent of the Owner, nor in time of war, but in a manner to be prescribed by law.

IV The right of the people to be secure in their persons, houses, papers and effects, against unreasonable searches and seizures, shall not be violated, and no Warrants shall issue, but upon probable cause, supported by Oath or affirmation, and particularly describing the place to be searched, and the persons or things to be seized.

V   No person shall be held to answer for a capital, or otherwise infamous crime, unless on a presentment or indictment of a Grand Jury, except in cases arising in the land or naval forces, or in the Militia, when in actual service in time of War or in public danger; nor shall any person be subject for the same offence to be twice put in jeopardy of life or limb; nor shall be compelled in any Criminal Case to be a witness against himself; nor be deprived of life, liberty, or property, without due process of law; nor shall private property be taken for public use, without just compensation.

VI In all criminal prosecutions, the accused shall enjoy the right to a speedy and public trial, by an impartial jury of the State and district wherein the crime shall have been committed, which district shall have been previously ascertained by law, and to be informed of the nature and cause of the accusation; to be confronted with the Witnesses against him; to have compulsory process for obtaining Witnesses in his favor, and to have the Assistance of Counsel for his defense.

VII In suits at common law, where the value in controversy shall exceed twenty dollars, the right of trial by jury shall be preserved, and no fact tried by a jury shall be otherwise re-examined in any Court of the United States, than according to the rules of the common law.

VIII Excessive bail shall not be required, nor excessive fines imposed, nor cruel and unusual punishments inflicted.

IX The enumeration in the Constitution, of certain rights, shall not be construed to deny or disparage others retained by the people.

X The powers not delegated to the United States by the Constitution, nor prohibited by it to the States, are reserved to the States respectively, or to the people.

Q. Who writes amendments to the Constitution and who votes on them?

A. Amendments to the Constitution may be written and proposed by either the U.S. Senate or the House of Representatives. In order to become a permanent addition to the Constitution, the amendment must be ratified by three-fourths of the nation's states.

How to Do Legal Research

Interested in the law? Legal research? Public libraries and law libraries aren't to be feared—only tackled. Finding a particular law or legal article isn't difficult. Can you imagine adding to your term paper one of these easy-to-find resources in support of your position? Follow the simple instructions offered here, and you'll be ready to present your case.

The published opinions of all of the country's appellate courts are found in a series of books called *Reporters*. The series is divided into regions—for example, California decisions are found in the *Pacific Reporter*, and Vermont decisions are located in the *Atlantic Reporter*. Each state also maintains its own set of reports. This means that each decision may be found in both a regional and a state report. The decisions of the U.S. Supreme Court can be found in at least four different *Reporters*. All of the Supreme Court cases cited in this book are also located in either the *U.S. Supreme Court Reports* or the *Supreme Court Reporter*.

Each published opinion is assigned a citation number. For example, if you want to read the full opinion of the U.S. Supreme Court in *Vernonia School District v. Jimmy Acton* (1995), you start with the case citation, which is 515 U.S. 646 (1995). This means you can find the opinion in volume 515 of the *U.S. Supreme Court Reports*, on page 646; 1995 refers to the year of the decision.

Take the case of *Rachel Kingsley v. Gregory Kingsley* (1993) as another example. Its citation is 623 So.2d 780 (1993). This isn't a U.S. Supreme Court case; its published opinion may be found in volume 623 of the *Southern Reporter* (abbreviated So.), second series, on page 780. Legal articles are located in the same way. Their citations usually list the name of the journal publishing the article, a volume number followed by the page number, and the year the article was written. On pages 21–28, you'll find a list of citations for the cases featured in *Teens Take It to Court*.

If there isn't a law library in your area, you can write to the near-est one, whether in your state or in a neighboring state. Provide the name and citation of the case or article you'd like, so a librarian can assist you. You may have to pay a small fee for photocopies. You can find information on some cases, particularly Supreme Court cases on the Web site FindLaw, *www.findlaw.com.*

The information is public, meaning it's available for your use. You don't have to be a judge, lawyer, or law student to obtain this material.

STATE AND FEDERAL REPORTS, WITH ABBREVIATIONS

Atlantic Reporter (A)   *Pacific Reporter* (P)
Northwest Reporter (N.W.)   *Federal Reporter* (F)
Northeast Reporter (N.E.)   *Federal Supplement* (F.Supp.)
Southern Reporter (So.)   *U.S. Supreme Court Reports* (U.S.)
Southwest Reporter (S.W.)   *Supreme Court Reporter* (S.Ct.)
Southeast Reporter (S.E.)

Note: A "2d" or "3d" following any of these abbreviations means second or third series, which is printed on the side of the volume.

CITATIONS FOR CASES IN THIS BOOK

Case 1:

Rachel Kingsley v. Gregory Kingsley, 623 So.2d 780 (Florida, 1993)

In the Interest of R. D. and B. D., 658 So.2d 1378 (Mississippi, 1995)

Care and Protection of Georgette, 785 N.E.2d 356
(Massachusetts, 2003)

In re Williams, 805 N.E.2d 1110 (Ohio, 2004)

Adoption of F. R. F. and D. B. F., 870 P.2d 799 (Oklahoma, 1994)

J. A. R. v. Superior Court, 877 P.2d 1323 (Arizona, 1994)

Adoption of J., 642 N.Y.S.2d 814 (New York, 1996)

Case 2:

Meyer v. Nebraska, 262 U.S. 390 (Nebraska, 1923)

People v. Sisson, 2 N.E.2d 660 (New York, 1936)

Downen v. Testa, 2003 WL 2002411 (Tennessee, 2003)

Rust v. Reyer, 670 N.Y.S.2d 822 (New York, 1998)

E. W. R. v. State of Wyoming, 902 P.2d 696 (Wyoming, 1995)

People v. J. M., 22 P.3d 545 (Colorado, 2000)

City of St. Clair Shores v. Provenzino, Macomb County Circuit Court (Michigan, 1997)

Case 3:

Gebser v. Lago Vista Independent School District, 118 S.Ct. 2275 (Texas, 1998)

Davis v. Monroe County Board of Education, 526 U.S. 629 (Georgia, 1999)

Hawkins v. Sarasota County School Board, 322 F.3d 1279 (Florida, 2003)

Rowinsky v. Bryan Independent School District, 80 F.3d 1006 (Texas, 1996)

Vance v. Spencer County Public School District, 231 F.3d 253 (Kentucky, 2000)

Franklin v. Gwinnett County Public Schools, 503 U.S. 60 (Georgia, 1992)

Abeyta v. Chama Valley Independent School District, 77 F.3d 1253 (New Mexico, 1996)

Case 4:

Beth Ann Faragher v. City of Boca Raton, 118 S.Ct. 2275 (Florida, 1998)

Meritor Savings Bank v. Mechelle Vinson, 477 U.S. 57 (District of Columbia, 1986)

Sunny Kim Smith v. Flagstar Corporation, 17 F.Supp.2d 1195 (Colorado, 1998)

Burlington Industries, Inc. v. Ellerth, 524 U.S. 742 (Illinois, 1998)

Joseph Oncale v. Sundowner Offshore Services, 523 U.S. 75 (Louisiana, 1998)

Case 5:

Vernonia School District v. Jimmy Acton, 515 U.S. 646 (Oregon, 1995)

Board of Education v. Earls, 122 S.Ct. 2559 (Oklahoma, 2002)

Anderson Community School Corps. v. Willis, 119 S.Ct. 1254 (Indiana, 1999)

Petersen v. City of Mesa, 83 P.3d 35 (Arizona, 2004)

M. C. English v. Talledega County Board of Education, 938 F.Supp. 775 (Alabama, 1996)

Chandler v. Miller, 520 U.S. 305 (Georgia, 1997)

New Jersey Local 304 v. New Jersey Transit, 701 A.2d 1243 (New Jersey, 1997)

Rebel v. Unemployment Compensation Board, 692 A.2d 304 (Pennsylvania, 1997)

Case 6:

New Jersey v. T. L. O., 469 U.S. 325 (New Jersey, 1985)

State v. Washington, 94 Wash.App. 1055 (Washington, 1999)

Jane Doe v. Little Rock School District, 380 F.3d 349 (Arkansas, 2004)

DesRoches v. Caprio, 156 F.3d 571 (Virginia, 1998)

Owasso v. Falvo, 534 U.S. 426 (Oklahoma, 2002)

Shade v. City of Farmington, 309 F.3d 1054 (Minnesota, 2002)

In re Roy L., 4 P.3d 984 (Arizona, 2000)

Commonwealth v. Cass, 666 A.2d 313 (Pennsylvania, 1995)

Doe v. Renfrow, 631 F.2d 91 (Indiana, 1980)

People v. Parker, 672 N.E.2d 813 (Illinois, 1996)

Oliver v. McClung, 919 F.Supp. 1206 (Indiana, 1995)

Case 7:

Tariq A-R Y v. Maryland, 118 S.Ct. 1105 (Maryland, 1998)

Hiibel v. Sixth Judicial District Court of Nevada, 124 S.Ct. 2451 (Nevada, 2004)

State v. Morrison, 56 P.3d 63 (Arizona, 2002)

Scheib v. Grant, 22 F.3d 149 (Illinois, 1994)

Florida v. J. L., 120 S.Ct. 1375 (Florida, 2000)

State v. Lowrimore, 841 P.2d 779 (Washington, 1992)

In re Bounmy V., 17 Cal.Rptr.2d 557 (California, 1993)

State v. Patterson, 868 A.2d 188 (Maine, 2005)

Wyoming v. Houghton, 526 U.S. 295 (Wyoming, 1999)

State v. Hauser, 464 S.E.2d 443 (North Carolina, 1995)

State v. Summers, 764 P.2d 250 (Washington, 1988)

State v. Carsey, 664 P.2d 1085 (Oregon, 1983)

Case 8:

Kent v. United States, 383 U.S. 541 (District of Columbia, 1966)

In re J. W., 804 N.E.2d 1094 (Illinois, 2004)

In re Abraham, 597 N.W.2d 836 (Michigan, 1999)

State v. Terry, 569 N.W.2d 364 (Iowa, 1997)

Appling v. State, 470 S.E.2d 761 (Georgia, 1996)

Case 9:

Bellotti v. Baird, 443 U.S. 622 (Massachusetts, 1979)

Roe v. Wade, 410 U.S. 113 (Texas, 1973)

In re Jane Doe, 645 N.E.2d 134 (Ohio, 1994)

Lambert v. Wicklund, 520 U.S. 292 (Montana, 1997)

Ayotte v. Planned Parenthood of Northern New England, S.Ct., 2006 WL 119149 (New Hampshire, 2006)

Parents United for Better Schools v. Philadelphia Board of Education, 978 F.Supp. 197 (Pennsylvania, 1997)

Doe v. Irwin, 615 F.2d 1162 (Michigan, 1980)

In re T. A. J., 73 Cal.Rptr.2d 331 (California, 1998)

Case 10:

Tinker v. Des Moines Independent School District, 393 U.S. 503 (Iowa, 1969)

In re George T., 93 P.3d 1007 (California, 2004)

Bethel School District v. Fraser, 478 U.S. 675 (Washington, 1986)

Cecilia Lacks v. Ferguson School District, 154 F.3d 904
(Missouri, 1999)

Lovell v. Poway Unified School District, 90 F.3d 367 (California, 1996)

Walker-Serrano v. Leonard, 325 F.3d 412 (Pennsylvania, 2003)

Broussard v. School Board of City of Norfolk, 801 F.Supp. 1526
(Virginia, 1992)

Newsom v. Albemarle County School Board, 354 F.3d 249
(Virginia, 2003)

Pyle v. School Commission, 667 N.E.2d 869 (Massachusetts, 1996)

Denno v. School Board of Volusia County, 959 F.Supp. 1481
(Florida, 1997)

City of Harvard v. Todd Gaut, 660 N.E.2d 259 (Illinois, 1996)

Texas v. Johnson, 491 U.S. 397 (Texas, 1989)

Chandler v. McMinnville School District, 978 F.2d 524 (Oregon, 1992)

Case 11:

Olff v. East Side Union High School District, 404 U.S. 1042
(California, 1972)

Littlefield v. Forney Independent School District, 268 F.3d 275
(Texas, 2001)

Bastrop Independent School District v. Zachariah Toungate, 922 S.W.2d
650 (Texas, 1996)

Austin Barber v. Colorado Independent School District, 901 S.W.2d 447
(Texas, 1995)

Hines v. Caston School, 651 N.E.2d 330 (Indiana, 1995)

Richard Bivens v. Albuquerque Public Schools, 899 F.Supp. 556
(New Mexico, 1995)

Case 12:

Hazelwood School District v. Kuhlmeier, 484 U.S. 260 (Missouri, 1988)

In re Douglas D., 626 N.W.2d 725 (Wisconsin, 2001)

Beussink v. Woodland School District, 30 F.Supp.2d 1175 (Missouri, 1998)

Yeo v. Town of Lexington, 131 F.3d 241 (Massachusetts, 1997)

Boucher v. School Board of Greenfield, 134 F.3d 821 (Wisconsin, 1998)

Bystrom v. Fridley High School, 822 F.2d 747 (Minnesota, 1987)

Case 13:

Lee v. Weisman, 505 U.S. 577 (Rhode Island, 1992)

Jones v. Clear Creek School District, 977 F.2d 963 (Texas, 1992)

Santa Fe Independent School District v. Jane Doe, 530 U.S. 290 (Texas, 2000)

Hsu v. Roslyn Union Free School District, 876 F.Supp. 445 (New York, 1996)

Westside Community Board of Education v. Mergens, 496 U.S. 226 (Nebraska, 1990)

The Good News Club v. Milford Central Schools, 533 U.S. 98 (New York, 2001)

Hemry v. School Board of Colorado Springs, 760 F.Supp. 856 (Colorado, 1991)

Hills v. Scottsdale Unified School District, 329 F.3d 1044 (Arizona, 2004)

Muller v. Jefferson Lighthouse School, 98 F.3d 1530 (Wisconsin, 1996)

Metzel v. Leininger, 57 F.3d 618 (Illinois, 1995)

Board of Trustees of Jackson School v. Knox, 688 So.2d 778 (Mississippi, 1997)

Case 14:

Ingraham v. Wright, 430 U.S. 651 (Florida, 1977)

Goss v. Lopez, 419 U.S. 565 (Ohio, 1975)

Holbrook v. Commonwealth of Kentucky, 925 S.W.2d 191 (Kentucky, 1996)

D. B. v. Clarke County Board of Education, 469 S.E.2d 438 (Georgia, 1996)

Fuller v. Decatur Public School Board, 78 F.Supp.2d 812 (Illinois, 2000)

R. M. and B. C. v. Washakie County School District, 102 P.3d 868 (Wyoming, 2004)

Case 15:

Joshua DeShaney v. Winnebago County Social Services, 489 U.S. 189 (Wisconsin, 1989)

In re A. O., 2002 WL 1973910 (Iowa, 2002)

State v. Arnold, 543 N.W.2d 600 (Iowa, 1996)

Hildreth v. Iowa D. H. S., 550 N.W.2d 157 (Iowa, 1996)

In re Phillip B., 92 Cal.App.3d 796 (California, 1979)

Case 16:

Parham v. J. R., 442 U.S. 584 (Georgia, 1979)

R. J. D. v. Vaughan Clinic, 572 So.2d 1225 (Alabama, 1990)

Tate v. State, 864 So.2d 44 (Florida, 2003)

Case 17:

Parkerson v. Brooks, 516 U.S. 942 (Georgia, 1995)

Troxel v. Granville, 530 U.S. 57 (Washington, 2000)

In re Adoption of Pierce, 790 N.E.2d 680 (Massachusetts, 2003)

Crouse v. Crouse, 552 N.W.2d 413 (South Dakota, 1996)

E. N. O. v. L. M. M., 711 N.E.2d 886 (Massachusetts, 1999)

In the Interest of Baron, 670 So.2d 357 (Louisiana, 1996)

Riepe v. Riepe, 91 P.3d 312 (Arizona, 2004)

D. F. S. v. Ellis, 870 S.W.2d 463 (Missouri, 1994)

Hede v. Gilstrap, 107 P.3d 158 (Wyoming 2005)

W. G. T. v. B. C., 675 So.2d 1023 (Florida, 1996)

State v. Waters, 951 P.2d 317 (Washington, 1998)

Case 18:

In re Gault, 387 U.S. 1 (Arizona, 1967)

In re Andre M., 88 P.3d 552 (Arizona, 2004)

Yarborough v. Alvarado, 124 S.Ct. 2140 (California, 2004)

Commonwealth v. Ira I., 791 N.E.2d 894 (Massachusetts, 2003)

People v. Montanez, 652 N.E.2d 1271 (Illinois, 1995)

In re V. L. T., 686 N.E.2d 49 (Illinois, 1997)

Case 19:

Josh Davis v. Alaska, 415 U.S. 308 (Alaska, 1974)

State in the Interest of N. P., 544 So.2d 51 (Louisiana, 1989)

State v. LaMunyon, 911 P.2d 151 (Kansas, 1996)

Appeal in Maricopa County Juvenile No. JV-512600, 930 P.2d 496 (Arizona, 1997)

Wideman v. Garbarino, 770 P.2d 320 (Arizona, 1989)

In re Washington Post, 247 F.Supp.2d 761 (District of Columbia, 2003)

Case 20:

McKeiver v. Pennsylvania, 403 U.S. 528 (Pennsylvania, 1971)

Welfare of J. K. B., 552 N.W.2d 732 (Minnesota, 1996)

State v. Reynolds, 857 P.2d 842 (Oregon, 1993)

U.S. v. Nachtigal, 507 U.S. 1 (California, 1993)

Case 21:

Roper v. Simmons, 125 S.Ct. 1183 (Missouri, 2005)

Atkins v. Virginia, 536 U.S. 304 (Virginia, 2002)

People v. Launsburry, 551 N.W.2d 460 (Michigan, 1996)

Naovarath v. State, 779 P.2d 944 (Nevada, 1989)

State v. Eric Mitchell, 577 N.W.2d 481 (Minnesota, 1998)

State v. Pilcher, 655 So.2d 636 (Louisiana, 1995)

Check out the bibliography on pages 198–203 for more sources that may be of help.

Part 2:
The Cases

ISSUE:

Can you go to court on your own to protect your rights?

Case: *Rachel Kingsley v. Gregory Kingsley* (1993)

The Constitution and the laws of our country protect **minors** and adults alike. It only makes sense then that teens can go to court to make sure these rights are enforced and protected. When teens challenge a law or a policy, however, they're usually joined in the lawsuit by a parent or a **guardian,** who files the lawsuit on the minor's behalf. This case, which was initiated by a minor, challenges this custom.

THE FACTS

In a Florida case that gained national attention, eleven-year-old Gregory Kingsley asked a court to "divorce" his parents. Although the case wasn't really a divorce case, it had a similar effect. Gregory had lived in the same foster home for three years, after being abandoned by his parents. Now he wanted a new mom and dad, and he filed his own **petition** with the court to legally end his relationship with his biological parents. He also requested to be adopted by his foster family.

Gregory's birth father was an alcoholic and was physically abusive. He didn't fight the lawsuit. Gregory's mother, though, refused to give up her parental rights and asked for custody of Gregory. She also argued that, as a child, Gregory couldn't file a lawsuit. The evidence showed she was a neglectful parent and she abused alcohol, used drugs, and hadn't made contact with Gregory for almost two years.

YOU BE THE JUDGE

- Did Gregory have a right to bring his case to court by himself? What do you think?

- Should the case have been dismissed because Gregory was a minor? Why or why not?

THE RULING

The Florida Court of Appeals stood by tradition and held that Gregory couldn't sue on his own behalf. The court discussed the concept of **capacity to sue** as the ability of a person to come into court under his or her own name—a right that's generally limited to adults and minors who have **emancipation.**

Some states allow minors to appear in court with their parents or a guardian, and no attorney, on certain types of cases: truancy, name changes, adoptions, minor traffic citations. It's a state-by-state or even county-by-county policy.

The Florida court explained that minors are required to appear in court with an attorney, so the proceeding can move forward with the least amount of confusion and delay. The court also said that it's in the minor's best interests to have the guidance of someone familiar with the complexities of the law and the legal process.

In 1995, the Mississippi Supreme Court commented on the purpose of minors being represented in court: "Children are best served by a vigorous advocate free to investigate, consult with them at length, marshal evidence, and to **subpoena** and **cross-examine** witnesses," as well as guard the child's best interests. *In the Interest of R. D. and B. D.* (1995)

Consequently, the Florida judges agreed with Gregory's mother that her son didn't have a right to go to court on his own behalf. However, although Gregory couldn't seek a termination of his parents' rights on his own, someone else could file *for* him. In fact, four other petitions for termination were filed—by his foster father, his foster mother, a guardian, and the state department that had placed Gregory in foster care. So Gregory's petition, although unlawful, was considered harmless, because the others were legal.

The key issue before the court was what was in Gregory's best interests—who he'd live with—regardless of how the case was presented in the news. The press played this up as "child divorces his parents," which made for great headlines. However, this case was a routine termination proceeding, unique only because Gregory asked for it on his own.

Gregory's legal relationship with his biological parents was terminated, and he was adopted by his foster parents.

RELATED CASES

Gregory's case raises the question of how teens can exercise and protect their rights. The decision in this case doesn't limit minors' rights; it only establishes that children and teens must be accompanied in their legal action by an adult—either a parent or a guardian. The following cases demonstrate why courts  consider it important for minors to be represented by either a lawyer or a **guardian ad litem.**

• What if the child's attorney disagrees with the wishes of the child?

When Georgette was eight years old, she and her brother and five sisters were removed from their father's home because of abuse and neglect. Georgette and her siblings were appointed a lawyer. After extensive efforts to reunite the family, the state sought to end the parents' rights and place the children in the permanent custody of the state. Their father objected and a court date was set. At the time of trial, Georgette, now thirteen, told her lawyer she wanted to live with her father again. Her lawyer informed the court of this but also argued it was in the best interest of all the children to remain in foster care or be adopted. He presented overwhelming evidence that the father had failed to change during the six years the children were in foster care, and won the case. Georgette and one of her siblings **appealed** this decision, arguing that their attorney had a conflict of interest in presenting a position different from theirs. The higher Massachusetts court ruled that Georgette and her siblings were entitled to an attorney and to have that attorney present their position to the court. However, the attorney is not always bound by a minor's decision when he or she feels it is not in the minor's best interests.

Care and Protection of Georgette (2003)

• Can children have a lawyer if their parents are facing termination of parental rights?

Malcolm was four when he was placed in foster care. He had witnessed a number of physical fights between his parents. His father had a history of criminal behavior and psychological disorders. His mother was neglectful, unemployed, and depressed. The state filed to terminate their parental rights. Malcolm was six at the time and wanted to return to his mother. The court terminated the rights of both parents. Malcolm's mother appealed, arguing that Malcolm should have had his own attorney to present his position in the case. The Ohio Supreme Court agreed, stating that in certain circumstances a child is entitled to independent counsel.

In re Williams (2004)

• Should children be represented by their own lawyer in an adoption case?

In Oklahoma, parents who don't financially support their child for twelve months may lose their parental rights. Tonya and Frank Foote had two children, F. R. F. and D. B. F. When the Footes divorced in 1990, the children were placed in Frank's custody and Tonya was ordered to pay child support. Frank later remarried, and his new wife wanted to adopt the children. Tonya hadn't met her child support obligations, but she didn't want her children to be adopted by their stepmother. The children weren't represented at the adoption hearing, which the Oklahoma appeals court ruled as essential. The court said if parents have a right to be represented when faced with losing their child, then the child—who's in the center of the case—has equal interests at stake and must also be represented.

Adoption of F. R. F. and D. B. F. (1994)

• What about custody proceedings? Do children have a right to their own lawyers in these cases?

J. A. R. was a seven-year-old in Arizona. For most of his life, his parents had been fighting over custody of him. He went back and forth between them, was interviewed by numerous mental health experts, and at one point was even kidnapped and taken to Mexico by his mother. Finally, the boy asked for his own attorney to speak for him alone. Although originally denied by the trial court because he already had a psychologist who'd look out for his best interests, the boy's request was later granted. A higher court—the Arizona Court of Appeals—concluded: "Children as young as five or six years of age, and certainly those of ten or twelve, are regarded as having opinions that are entitled to weight in legal proceedings concerning their custody."

J. A. R. v. Superior Court (1994)

• Do the circumstances of a gay adoption case affect a child's right to representation?

In a case in New York, X (the same-sex life partner of Y) wanted to adopt Y's baby, who was born through artificial insemination. X and Y had been together for eight years, and the baby's mother agreed to her partner's adoption of the baby. The court ruled that because this case involved special circumstances (same-sex adoption in New York was a relatively new event—approved by the courts in the early 1990s), the child needed to be represented in the proceedings. The court said the best interests of the child dictate whether he or she should have an attorney or a guardian in an adoption case.

This case points out the discrepancies in legal reasoning. Some courts rule one way, while other courts rule the opposite—all on the same set of facts, and all justified on the basis of what's in the child's best interests. This is why appellate courts exist: to review the decision of lower courts and make a final decision.

Adoption of J. (1996)

GET ON THE CASE

- Although, as a teen, you aren't allowed to go to court on your own, there are plenty of other ways to resolve conflicts or to ensure you're being treated properly. Make a list of the methods that you currently use to solve problems and conflicts with others. Then write down why these methods do or don't work for you. Now commit to discovering new ways to solve problems and to improve your conflict-resolution skills.

- Find out if your school has a peer mediation program to help resolve conflicts. If not, ask your principal or dean if you can work on developing one. If your school does have a peer mediation program, find out how you can get involved. Conflict-resolution skills are also taught through many community service organizations.

ISSUE:

Do your parents have the right to control your education?

Case: *Meyer v. Nebraska* (1923)

Almost every U.S. Supreme Court decision on teen rights and family law has relied in part on the decision of this 1923 case. Although the case is about a single issue—parents' rights to make decisions about their children's education—the ruling can be applied to many other types of cases in our changing society.

The next time you hear about a law concerning the rights and responsibilities of parents, or the rights and responsibilities of children to their parents, you can try to find a connection to this case.

THE FACTS

Ten-year-old Raymond Parpart attended Zion Parochial School in Hamilton County, Nebraska. Raymond's teacher, Robert T. Meyer, taught a Bible study class for a half hour each day. The class was taught in German, the native language of most of the community members. (Raymond spoke English as a first language.) Although students weren't required to attend Meyer's class, it was full. The purpose of the class was both to teach students German and to familiarize them with Bible stories.

A 1919 Nebraska law forbade teaching anyone in a foreign language, unless that person had finished eighth grade (which Raymond hadn't). The law was intended to encourage people to speak in the English language, so it would become the mother tongue of the state of Nebraska. Raymond's parents, however, wanted their son to learn a second language while he was young. The state of Nebraska charged the teacher with breaking the law.

YOU BE THE JUDGE

- Do you think Mr. Meyer was breaking the law if the students weren't required to attend the class? Why or why not?

- Who should decide what's best for each student in the class-room? Parents, teachers, or the government? Why?

- What role should parents play in their child's education? How much authority should they have?

THE RULING

The Nebraska trial court and the Nebraska Supreme Court found Mr. Meyer guilty of breaking the law. The penalty included a fine of $25 to $100, or thirty days in jail. He **appealed** his conviction, and the

U.S. Supreme Court ruled in Mr. Meyer's favor several years later. The Court decided that parents have a say in their children's education and that a state law that interferes with such a right is invalid. As a result, the prosecution by the state against the teacher for violating a law that was invalid had to be set aside; the conviction and penalty were vacated by the Supreme Court.

This "English only" debate has come full circle. Raymond's case took place in the 1920s. More than eight decades later, the debate continues in legislatures and in voting booths across the country. Several states have attempted to pass legislation requiring English to be the official language of the state. This would restrict speech and written documents in the public sector to English. Courts have been asked to decide the constitutionality of English-only laws, and so far have ruled against them. You may have the chance to vote on this issue in your own state.

In making its decision, the U.S. Supreme Court balanced the right of individual freedom with the legitimate interest of a state to protect its citizens. The Court found no harm to anyone in teaching elementary schoolchildren a foreign language. In fact, the Court emphasized the right, duty, and obligation of parents to be involved with the education of their children. The Supreme Court determined that the state, in passing a law that prohibited the teaching of a second language in public school, erred—that this was stepping into the private domain of parents' rights in raising their children. It wrote: "Corresponding to the right of control, it is the natural duty of the parent to give his children education suitable to their station in life. . . . The protection of the Constitution extends to all, to those who speak other languages as well as to those born with English on the tongue." The Court also spoke of a student's right to acquire knowledge, a teacher's right to teach, and the parents' power to control their child's education.

The principles outlined in the *Meyer* decision have been applied for more than eighty years, and with good reason. First, parents have both rights and responsibilities toward their children. Second, children and teens also have certain rights and responsibilities toward each other, their parents, and others. Schools aren't obligated to instill values in students. The laws and courts of this country recognize the family as the primary source of shaping and developing values in children.

Clarifying its limited role in family matters, a New York court ruled: "The court cannot regulate . . . the internal affairs of the home. Dispute between parents when it does not involve anything immoral or harmful to the welfare of the child is beyond the reach of the law. The vast majority of matters concerning the upbringing of children must be left to the conscience, patience, and self-restraint of father and mother. No end of difficulties would arise should judges try to tell parents how to bring up their children." *People v. Sisson* (1936)

RELATED CASES

You're probably aware that your parents have obligations and responsibilities when raising you. But did you know your behavior reflects on your parents—and they can be held legally accountable for what you do?

• Can your parents be held responsible for the consequences of hosting a party for young people with alcohol?

Michael and Carol Testa threw a high school graduation party for their daughter and her friends. They provided a keg of beer and served wine. Concerned about drinking and driving, the Testas initially collected the car keys of the kids who drove. However, as the Testas drank more and played drinking games with the kids, they stopped taking the keys. Later that night, two boys who had attended the party were involved in an accident. The driver was intoxicated and his passenger died in the accident. The Testas knew the risks of serving alcohol to teens who would be driving home. They voluntarily took steps to protect them by taking their keys but failed to follow through with all of the teens. As the social hosts of the party, they were ruled liable for these unintended consequences.

Downen v. Testa (2003)

• Are your parents responsible for your actions when they're not present?

In 1998, Carol Rust and Stephen Tarantino (both **minors**) went to a keg party at the house of seventeen-year-old Heidi Reyer in Merrick, New York. Heidi's parents were out of town for the weekend, and she agreed to allow a local fraternity to sell beer at a party in the Reyer home, in exchange for a cut of the money earned. Approximately 150 underage kids showed up and paid a fee to get in and drink as much beer as they wanted. The neighbors complained, and the police broke up the party.

Stephen had consumed quite a bit of beer and, while in the street in front of Heidi's house, punched Carol in the face and injured her. Carol sued Stephen, Heidi, and Heidi's parents. Because Heidi was a **minor,** her parents were named in the lawsuit—parents are liable under the law for the acts of their children. Heidi's parents argued that they weren't responsible, because their daughter hadn't supplied the beer or caused anyone at the party to become intoxicated. Under laws that make parents responsible for the unlawful acts of minors, the court ruled that liability exists for "those who knowingly furnish alcoholic beverages to underage persons at graduation parties, church socials, wedding receptions, office parties, and college campuses." Although Heidi's parents didn't furnish the alcohol, they could be held responsible because the party was held in their home, hosted by their underage daughter.

Rust v. Reyer (1998)

• Can your parents be sentenced as part of your sentence?

E. W. R., a Wyoming resident, was found guilty of a crime in 1993. His mother, his stepfather, and his father all attended his sentencing hearing, where he was given **probation** and counseling. In an effort to help the family work through some of the problems that had contributed to E. W. R.'s running away several times, the court ordered his parents to attend parenting classes. Held once a week over an

eight-week period, these classes were designed to be flexible, so people could attend around their work schedules and family commitments. E. W. R.'s father, E. L. R., didn't go to any of the classes. After several attempts to persuade him to attend, the court found him in **contempt of court** and sentenced him to thirty days in jail.
E. W. R. v. State of Wyoming (1995)

After J. M. missed several appointments with his **probation officer** because his father failed to arrange for his transportation, a Colorado court sentenced the father to two days in jail unless he helped his son succeed on probation. The sentence was later vacated by an appeals court, which ruled that the Colorado juvenile court didn't have **jurisdiction** over the father. People v. J. M. (2000)

• Can your parents be held criminally responsible for your actions?

Sixteen-year-old Alex Provenzino and his parents, Anthony and Susan, lived in St. Clair Shores, Michigan. In 1995, Alex was arrested for robbery, assault of his father, and a string of home burglaries. When the police searched Alex's room, they found a stolen handgun and marijuana on his nightstand. Alex was found guilty and sentenced to one year in a **detention** home.

The case didn't close here, however. Alex's parents were charged with violating the city's parent-responsibility law—specifically failing to prevent Alex from committing the burglaries. Anthony and Susan were found guilty by a jury and were ordered to pay $2,200 in fines and court costs, plus approximately $13,000 for Alex's care in the detention home.

Note: Alex's parents appealed their conviction and eventually were acquitted. The appeals court found that the parent-responsibility law was constitutional but that the charges against the Provenzinos—particularly the charge that they failed to get their son into counseling—weren't proven beyond a reasonable doubt.
City of St. Clair Shores v. Provenzino (1997)

Many states now have parent-responsibility laws. The increase in juvenile crime has caused state legislatures not only to study the problem but also to pass laws placing greater accountability on parents. Consequences for parents violating these laws include community service work, fines, parent-training classes, counseling, and, in some states, jail time.

GET ON THE CASE

- Did you ever think you could cause major legal problems for your mom or dad? To the point where one or both of them could go to jail for something you've done? Is this fair? Should your parents have to pay for your mistakes or share in the consequences? Why or why not? Do you think age should matter in this decision—for example, whether you're eleven or seventeen? Why?

- How involved are your parents in your education? Do you think they share responsibility for how you do in school? Would you like them to be more or less involved? Why?

What if you're sexually harassed at school?

Case: *Gebser v. Lago Vista Independent School District* (1998)

Sexual harassment isn't new. This type of abuse has been going on for years, and both males and females have been victimized by it. However, we now live in a time when this behavior is no longer overlooked or tolerated by society. Today, courts give you the right to seek damages (money) for your mental or physical suffering. While money isn't a *solution,* would-be harassers who know they can be held financially responsible for their actions may think twice about committing these offenses.

THE FACTS

In the spring of 1991, thirteen-year-old Alida Star Gebser was an eighth-grade honor student in Lago Vista, Texas. Her teacher, Trudy Waldrop, recommended that she join a book discussion group at the local high school led by her husband, Frank Waldrop (a teacher of advanced social studies). During some of the sessions, Mr. Waldrop made sexually suggestive comments to the book group. In the fall, Alida started high school and had Mr. Waldrop for classes both semesters that year. He continued to make inappropriate remarks to Alida in class, when alone with her in the classroom, and at her home, where he was mentoring her. (Alida later testified that she knew Mr. Waldrop's behavior was improper, but she didn't know what to do. His class was the school's only advanced program, and she wanted to stay in it.)

> Sexual harassment at school refers to any unwelcome sexual advances, requests for sexual favors, or other verbal or physical contact of a sexual nature. To be unlawful, it must be so offensive and severe that the conduct affects or disrupts the victim's education.

Over the next year, this student-teacher relationship progressed to kissing, fondling, and eventually sexual intercourse. Alida didn't report Mr. Waldrop's behavior. The parents of two other students complained to the school principal about the comments the teacher made in class. Then in early 1993, a police officer discovered Alida and Mr. Waldrop having sex in a parked car. Mr. Waldrop was fired and his teaching license was revoked.

Alida and her mother sued Mr. Waldrop and the school district, claiming **negligence** and **discrimination** based on sex. In other words, Alida argued that she was treated differently by Mr. Waldrop because she was a girl. Alida and her mother also held the school district responsible for failing to prevent the teacher's misconduct.

YOU BE THE JUDGE

- Should the school district be held responsible for Mr. Waldrop's behavior? Why or why not?

- Does it matter whether the school knew about the teacher's behavior?

THE RULING

The federal court of appeals dismissed the lawsuit against the school district and sent the case back to the trial court for a decision against Mr. Waldrop. Alida **appealed** to the U.S. Supreme Court which, in a five to four decision, agreed with the lower court.

This was a close decision that, at first glance, may surprise you. How could a school district not be held responsible for the behavior of one of its teachers? (Especially over a lengthy period of misconduct, affecting not just one, but a number of students.) Whose responsibility is it to protect students from adult predators? These are good questions, without easy answers.

The U.S. Supreme Court based its decision on a narrow, limited interpretation of what Congress intended when it passed Title 9 of the Education Amendments in 1972. This is a federal law aimed at protecting individuals from discrimination on the basis of sex. The law specifically prohibits discrimination in any educational program or activity that receives federal money. This includes all public schools.

The Court didn't rule that school districts were responsible for every discriminatory act of its employees (teachers, administrators, etc.). School districts can't be held accountable for sexual harassment by a teacher against a student if the incident isn't reported or known by the school district. Although sexual harassment may be discrimination on the basis of sex, the school district must know about the misconduct and have an opportunity to remedy it. If the district knows about the behavior and does nothing, *then* it may be held responsible.

Otherwise, if action is taken—as in this case, where Mr. Waldrop was fired and his license revoked—the school district isn't liable for damages to Alida. (Liability, in this instance, means being legally responsible for any expenses Alida had as a result of the teacher's harassment, such as counseling or medication.) The Court pointed out that the school district wasn't informed of the sexual harassment incidents during the months of misconduct. The principal was only told about the inappropriate comments made by Mr. Waldrop in class and, once the teacher was caught with Alida, immediate action was taken.

The Court said its decision wasn't meant to prevent Alida and her mother from suing Mr. Waldrop as an *individual*. The family just couldn't sue the school district under the federal Education Law or in federal court.

Four of the U.S. Supreme Court justices disagreed with the majority opinion. In a **dissenting opinion,** Justice John Paul Stevens wrote: "As long as school boards can insulate themselves from knowledge about this sort of conduct, they can claim immunity from damages liability." (In other words, schools shouldn't be allowed to claim ignorance of misconduct and thereby avoid responsibility.)

Justice Sandra Day O'Connor wrote the majority decision, concluding with this statement: "The number of reported cases involving sexual harassment of students in schools confirms that harassment unfortunately is an all too common aspect of the educational experience. No one questions that a student suffers extraordinary harm when subjected to sexual harassment and abuse by a teacher, and that the teacher's conduct is reprehensible and undermines the basic purposes of the educational system."

As a result of this case, public schools across the country are working to develop sexual harassment policies and make sure staff and students are aware of them. Students have a right to be free from sex discrimination, and schools have a duty to take reasonable steps to prevent and be aware of all forms of harassment.

RELATED CASES

Over the past decade, great advances have been made in the laws regarding individual rights, whether one is a **minor** or an adult. You can seek protection from someone who's violating your rights, as well as take action for physical, emotional, or psychological injuries. The law even covers peer harassment, if it's severe and disrupts your education.

• Can schools be held responsible when students harass each other?

Ten-year-old LaShonda Davis was sexually harassed by fifth-grader G. F. in Monroe County, Georgia. LaShonda's mother complained to her daughter's teacher and to the principal, but nothing was done. It took the school three months to move G. F.'s desk away from LaShonda's. G. F. was charged with sexual battery and admitted his behavior in court. LaShonda and her mother filed a discrimination suit against the school board for failing to protect LaShonda from student-on-student sexual harassment. The U.S. Supreme Court ruled, five to four, that school districts may be held responsible for failing to stop student-on-student sexual harassment. If the school knows about the harassment, it must take reasonable steps to stop it. This case extended the protection against sexual harassment from teacher-on-student to student-on-student harassment.

Davis v. Monroe County Board of Education (1999)

• Does it matter how soon problems are reported?

An eight-year-old second-grade boy made sexual comments and gestures to female classmates. The harassment started at the beginning of the 1998–1999 school year. When the school learned of the harassment in May 1999, the boy was suspended for one week. A month later, he was suspended for the remainder of the school year due to new incidents and was required to attend counseling during the summer. In 2000, three of the students and their parents filed a lawsuit against the Sarasota County School Board alleging that their daughters were the victims of sexual harassment by the second-grade student. The federal trial court dismissed the case and this decision was affirmed by the appellate court. The girls' lawsuit for student-on-student harassment was dismissed because they weren't specific in their reporting of the incidents and they waited months before telling anyone. Also, there was no evidence that their grades declined or their demeanor or classroom participation changed in any way.

Hawkins v. Sarasota County School Board (2003)

• If a school knows about harassment between students and tries to correct the problem, can it still be held responsible?

Between September 1992 and March 1993, sisters Jane and Janet Doe (not their real names) from Bryan, Texas, were sexually assaulted a number of times by boys on the school bus and in class. The bus driver and administration were told of the incidents, and the girls' mother filed a complaint. The boys were briefly suspended from riding the bus and attending school. Jane and Janet's mother sued the school district for damages. The Fifth Circuit Court of Appeals dismissed the case, stating that the school couldn't be held responsible for the student-on-student harassment because the boys had been disciplined in the same manner as girls would be—in other words, in a nondiscriminatory way, which was correct under the law.

Rowinsky v. Bryan Independent School District (1996)

• Can you sue the school district for failing to prevent an abusive environment?

Upon transferring to a new school in sixth grade, Alma was victimized by her peers for the next three years. She was propositioned and touched inappropriately in all of her classes; she was hit by both boys and girls, shoved into walls, and had her homework stolen or destroyed. She was stabbed once with a pen and was rescued by a student from an attempted sexual assault in one of her classes. Her mother repeatedly reported the incidents to the teachers and principal at the school in Taylorsville, Kentucky, but no action was taken against the offenders. Alma was diagnosed with depression and withdrew from school. She and her family then sued the school district for intentional sexual discrimination as a result of peer conduct, arguing that the school board was deliberately indifferent to the sexual harassment. A jury found in Alma's favor, awarding her $220,000 against the school board. The persistent verbal and physical sexual harassment effectively denied her an education.

Vance v. Spencer County Public School District (2000)

• Do schools need to protect students from sexual harassment?

Christine Franklin was in tenth grade at North Gwinnett High School in Georgia. Andrew Hill was a teacher and coach at the school. His harassment of Christine started with sexually oriented conversations and progressed to forcibly kissing her and calling her at home. On three occasions, he coerced her into intercourse in a private office at school. Christine reported Mr. Hill to the administration. He resigned from his job, with an understanding that the matter would be dropped.

Christine took her case to court, claiming intentional gender-based discrimination. Although she was no longer a student at the school and Mr. Hill no longer taught there, the U.S. Supreme Court ruled that her sexual harassment claim was valid and the suit would proceed. The Court indicated its unanimous position that schools have a responsibility to protect students.

Franklin v. Gwinnett County Public Schools (1992)

• What if your teacher is emotionally abusive? Is this a violation of your civil rights?

Twelve-year-old Stephanie Abeyta, a New Mexico student, wrote a note to fifth-grader Dominic saying, "You're cute . . . I like you." Stephanie's teacher found the note and read it to the class. He then asked the class if they thought Stephanie was a prostitute. Over the next three months, Stephanie's teacher and classmates continued to taunt her, until Stephanie changed schools. She and her parents filed a federal lawsuit against the teacher and the school district, alleging psychological abuse. Because Stephanie and her parents claimed that the teacher's actions violated her civil rights—the charges were sexual abuse and harassment, and psychological abuse—they brought their case to a federal court rather than starting out in state court. The Tenth Circuit Court of Appeals ruled that, although Stephanie's teacher emotionally abused her, his actions didn't amount to torture or severe psychological abuse. The court condemned the teacher's behavior but left the matter to be pursued in state court—not federal.

Abeyta v. Chama Valley Independent School District (1996)

GET ON THE CASE

- Have you experienced harassment similar to what is described in these cases? What did you do about it? Did you tell anyone or let it go? Would you do anything different now?

- Do you think schools have a duty to protect students from sexual harassment? If so, how can schools do this? What new precautions could your school take to protect students? What role should teachers, school administrators, parents, students, and security officers play in this matter?

- Read the daily newspaper closely for one month, clipping articles about sexual harassment. At the end of this period, sort through the clippings to see if you spot any trends. How many articles did you find on this subject? Compare how many articles were about harassment in the workplace versus in schools. How many involved minors versus adults? What do you learn from the trends you see? What might you do to address problems or unfair situations you discover?

- Does your school have a written sexual harassment policy? Check your school rules or school handbook for the section on sexual harassment and how to report it. (You could also ask an administrator or a school counselor for the policy.) If no handbook exists, most likely one is in the works as a result of the 1998 *Gebser* decision.

ISSUE:

What if you're sexually harassed at work?

Case: *Beth Ann Faragher v. City of Boca Raton* (1998)

Although teasing, flirting, and cracking jokes are okay in many job situations, at other times they're definitely inappropriate—and even illegal, as you'll see in this case. If you're ever a victim of **sexual harassment** at school, at work, or in the community, you're not alone or without recourse. It's important to understand what your rights are and what action you can take to protect yourself. The laws in this area have been expanded in recent years. Above all, know that you don't have to put up with such behavior by anyone, male or female.

THE FACTS

After graduating from high school, Beth decided to work her way through college as a lifeguard at the city beach in Boca Raton, Florida. She worked full time during the summers and part time during the school year. Throughout her five years as a lifeguard, she had several male supervisors. She worked with three to five other women; forty to fifty of the lifeguards were men. After finishing college, Beth quit her job and went on to graduate school.

Throughout her time as a lifeguard, Beth experienced "uninvited and offensive touching" and heard sexual comments from her supervisors. One of the supervisors threatened to make her clean the toilets for a year if she didn't date him. She refused. Although she didn't complain to anyone about what was going on, she filed a sexual harassment lawsuit against the city and the offending supervisors after leaving her job. Beth claimed that their acts created a hostile work environment, which amounted to employment **discrimination.** She also argued that the city failed to prevent the harassment.

YOU BE THE JUDGE

- Do you think the behavior of Beth's supervisors was sexual harassment?

- Is the city responsible for what happened among its employees? Why or why not?

THE RULING

While deciding whether to consider Beth's case, the U.S. Supreme Court reviewed the history of civil rights law and how it applies to the workplace. The Court determined that the Civil Rights Act of 1964 provides protection from sexual harassment at work. The act reads, in part: "It shall be an unlawful employment practice for an employer . . . to discriminate against any individual . . . because of . . . race, color, religion, sex, or national origin."

The Court, in a seven to two decision written by Justice David H. Souter, held that sexual harassment so severe as to create an abusive working environment is prohibited. The Court recognized that human behavior oftentimes leads to simple teasing, offhand comments, and even isolated incidents of abusive language or gender-related jokes. These, by themselves, aren't usually sufficient to claim sexual harassment. *Extreme* conduct, however, is what people are protected against.

The Court requires that all of the circumstances of the work environment be studied in determining whether harassment occurred. This includes (1) the frequency of the discriminating conduct, (2) its severity, (3) whether it's physically threatening or humiliating, and (4) whether it interferes with an employee's work performance. All of these factors are considered in a sexual harassment case—as well as whether the employer knew or should have known about the harassment.

Not every act of harassment is held against the owner of a business or company. The court considers whether the company has a specific policy against harassment and whether all employees are made aware of it. For example, when you start a job, you should be told about your right to raise an issue of harassment if one occurs. On the other hand, it's your duty as an employee to take reasonable care to avoid any harm from a harasser—for example, by reporting all incidents when they occur. (A victim isn't required to confront the abuser but needs to report the abuse to someone in authority, such as a supervisor.)

An earlier sexual discrimination case regarding a young bank teller and the bank manager in Washington, D.C., went to the U.S. Supreme Court in 1986. In a decision written by Justice William H. Rehnquist, it was decided that when a supervisor sexually harasses an employee because of the employee's sex, discrimination has occurred. The key to a sexual harassment claim isn't whether the victim voluntarily participated in sexual incidents with the offender, but whether the superior's advances were unwelcome. *Meritor Savings Bank v. Mechelle Vinson* (1986)

In Beth's case, the Court created a balancing test in sexual harassment incidents: between the reasonableness of the employer's conduct in seeking to prevent and correct harassing behavior, and the reasonableness of the employee's behavior in seeking to avoid harm. Because the city in Beth's case didn't make its lifeguards aware of its anti-harassment policy, the city was liable for the supervisors' acts. Beth was awarded $10,000 against her two supervisors, an additional $500 against one of the supervisors for punitive damages (money awarded to a victim, intended to punish the defendant), and $1 against the city of Boca Raton, which was found least liable for the supervisors' behavior. In addition, the city was told to make sure that all city employees are aware of its anti-harassment policy and to develop a sensible complaint procedure for victims of sexual harassment.

In discussing the responsibility of supervisors at work, the Court stated that a "supervisor is clearly charged with maintaining a productive, safe work environment. . . . A pervasively hostile work environment of sexual harassment is never (one would hope) authorized."

This case is significant because it establishes a standard for determining if certain conduct in the workplace is against the law. It helps employees and employers understand the limits of sexual comments and behavior at work—and helps make it clear that monetary damages are available against the offender *and* the place of employment.

Regardless of your age, you have rights at work. Offensive sexual language or gestures that create a hostile or abusive work environment don't have to be tolerated. As you enter the workforce, be aware that if you're harassed by someone on the job, you can do something about it. Putting up with the abuse allows it to continue—and spread to other victims.

RELATED CASES

Incidents of sexual harassment were ignored for many years, but today people are much more aware of the laws surrounding this issue. As a result, we're witnessing many changes and expansions in the protections against sexual harassment, including same-sex harassment.

• If you're harassed at work, do you need to take action right away?

At age fifteen, Sunny was hired as a hostess at a restaurant in Denver, Colorado. During her first month on the job, the restaurant manager allegedly sexually harassed and assaulted her. Sunny didn't report his behavior until after she voluntarily transferred to another restaurant the next month. Sunny was eventually fired for missing work and arriving late.

Sunny later sued the first restaurant and its manager for sexual harassment. The Colorado District Court dismissed the case in part because Sunny hadn't acted fast enough. The court considered the fact that she hadn't told anyone at the time of the incidents, that the restaurant hadn't taken action against her (by demoting or transferring her, for example), and that her eventual termination wasn't related to the sexual harassment claim.

Sunny Kim Smith v. Flagstar Corporation (1998)

• What if you quit the job? Can you still file a lawsuit against your employer?

Just out of college, Kimberly (age twenty-three) was hired as a salesperson for a large company in Chicago. Throughout her first year on the job, her supervisor subjected Kimberly to constant sexual harassment. He made remarks about her breasts, said he could make her life very hard or very easy, and told her she should loosen up and wear shorter skirts. During a promotion interview her supervisor reached over and rubbed her knee. Kimberly received the promotion and suffered no tangible retaliation from rejecting her supervisor's advances. However, after a year of this behavior she quit and filed a lawsuit against the company for creating a hostile work environment. Even though Kimberly didn't report the

incidents until after she left the job, the U.S. Supreme Court determined that she had a valid claim and allowed the case to proceed.
Burlington Industries, Inc. v. Ellerth (1998)

It's always best to act promptly if you're harassed at work, instead of letting a lot of time go by before reporting the incident; be sure to talk to someone in authority, too. You can go over your supervisor's head, if he or she is the harasser. Inform a higher-level manager or the owner of the establishment you work for. Here's a recommended plan of action:

1. Discuss the situation with your mom or dad.

2. Report the problem to an authority at work.

3. Contact the Equal Employment Opportunity Commission (EEOC) or state civil rights office.

4. Find out if the employer is willing to remedy the situation.

5. If the employer doesn't fix the problem, you may want to contact a lawyer and file a lawsuit.

• Is it sexual harassment if the person is the same sex as you?

Joseph Oncale, twenty-one, worked as a member of an eight-man crew on an oil derrick (tower) in the Gulf of Mexico. Three of his coworkers sexually harassed and threatened him. Joseph complained to the company's superiors, but no action was taken. He eventually quit due to "sexual harassment and verbal abuse." He sued the company, his supervisors, and his coworkers, claiming that harassment between members of the same sex is no different from discrimination among members of the opposite sex. The U.S. Supreme Court reviewed this Louisiana case and agreed, saying the law "protects men as well as women" in the workplace. The Court also said that sexual harassment laws provide protection only in cases where the behavior in question is so severe that it prevents the victim from doing his or her job. The Court, in a unanimous decision, indicated that common sense would help courts and juries distinguish between simple teasing or roughhousing and behavior that's severe enough to be called sexual harassment.
Joseph Oncale v. Sundowner Offshore Services (1998)

GET ON THE CASE

- Consider the following situations and discuss with your classmates or parents what you think about each.

Julie works at a fast-food restaurant after school and on weekends. Her boss promises her a raise—if she'll go out with him. Is this sexual harassment? What can Julie do in this situation?

Maya works as a cashier at a gas station. Some of the mechanics make sexual comments to her during the day, and their work area is covered with pictures of nude women. Maya's boss tells her to ignore these issues—that she's working in a "man's world" and she can either get used to it or find another job. Does Maya have any recourse? Can she, as the youngest person and the only female on the job, change her work environment without losing her source of employment? What would you recommend that she do?

Seventeen-year-old Craig is spending the summer working in his father's accounting office. The office manager is interested in him and asks him to meet her after work. She's also Craig's supervisor. Is this sexual harassment? Craig doesn't want to jeopardize his job or ruin his father's trust in him. How should he respond?

- What about when people who work together date each other? Do you think this has the potential to cause problems, or is it okay? Why? Does it matter whether the two people are on the same job level, or whether one is in a higher position than the other? Do you think employers can create rules about dating among employees?

- Create a poster or flyer to spread the word about sexual harassment in the workplace. Start by coming up with a list of behaviors that are inappropriate, and then cross them out or write "no" beside them. Be creative, using paints, markers, or other materials to make the poster eye-catching. Ask your teacher or principal if you can display the poster at school as a way to inform others; if you have a job, ask your boss to display the poster at work.

Do you have to be tested for drugs to try out for school sports?

Case: *Vernonia School District v. Jimmy Acton* (1995)

Underage drinking and drug use is a growing concern for schools—public and private—across the country. School districts are trying to combat this problem in many ways, including drug testing. Although such tests are yet to be required of an entire public school population, they're more frequently required of students who wish to participate in sports and other activities. The question is, does this rule violate a student's right to privacy? And is it fair to demand such a test for students in some school activities but not in others?

THE FACTS

James (Jimmy) Acton was a seventh-grader in Vernonia, Oregon. During the 1980s, this logging community of approximately 3,000 people witnessed a sharp increase in drug and alcohol use by students. Class disruptions and sports-related injuries due to the influence of drugs frequently occurred. Consequently, the school district developed a drug policy requiring student athletes to take a drug test at the beginning of the season and to submit to random testing throughout the year. Following a parent-input meeting, where unanimous approval was given, the policy went into effect in 1989.

In 1991, twelve-year-old Jimmy wanted to try out for the football team. Under the school's policy, he was given consent forms for drug testing, which he and his parents needed to sign. After talking about the issue at home, the family decided not to sign the forms. They explained to the principal, Randall Aultman, that they objected to the testing because there was no evidence that Jimmy used drugs or alcohol. Following the policy, the school suspended Jimmy from sports for the season. He and his parents filed a lawsuit against the school district, challenging the urinalysis requirement for sports participation. They argued that mandated, suspicionless drug testing is a search that violates the Fourth Amendment protection (see the **Bill of Rights** on pages 18–19) against unreasonable searches.

YOU BE THE JUDGE

- Do you think the school district's policy violated the Fourth Amendment—was it unreasonable to require all student athletes to be tested for drug use?

- The policy didn't call for drug testing of students who weren't active in sports. Do student athletes have fewer privacy rights than other students?

THE RULING

The question put to the U.S. Supreme Court was whether mandatory drug tests violated students' Fourth Amendment protection against unreasonable **search and seizure.** There's no question that drug testing, which is done by analyzing a blood or urine sample, is a personal search. So the issue is whether a student's right to privacy is more important than the school's job of keeping its campus safe and drug-free for all students.

> Drugs are more easily traced in urine than in blood. And because giving a urine sample is less "invasive" than having blood drawn, it's the more frequent method of drug testing.

The U.S. Supreme Court ruled that the school district policy was reasonable and constitutional based on (1) a student athlete's decreased expectation of privacy, (2) the limited invasion of privacy in obtaining a urine sample, and (3) the importance of the need met by the search, which was to reduce drug use by athletes. In a six to three decision, the Court said that any intrusion of a student's privacy by submitting to a drug test is minimal.

The Court also ruled that the protections provided in the testing procedures further supported their use. The tests were only for drugs—not, for example, to detect pregnancy or disease. In addition, the test results would be shared only with certain school employees; the results wouldn't be turned over to the police or be used for school disciplinary action. The school district had outlined very specific procedures: If a student tested positive, a second test would be conducted; if the second test was negative, the matter would be considered closed; if the second test came back positive, the parents and student would be notified. The student would then be required to complete a six-week outpatient drug-counseling program and be tested for drugs each week. After meeting these requirements, the student could return to sports. If the student refused the counseling or further drug tests, he or she would be suspended from all sports for the season.

In making its decision, the U.S. Supreme Court considered a student's expectation of privacy. You surrender some privacy when you go to school. Your parents turn over temporary custody to the school, for educational and disciplinary purposes when necessary. The school, in turn, is responsible for following laws that are intended to protect you. For example, they must conduct physical examinations, such as vision, hearing, and scoliosis tests. Schools also need to make sure students have had all of their immunizations. These requirements mean, in the eyes of the law, you can expect less privacy in school.

If you're a student athlete, you have even fewer privacy rights. By trying out for a team, you agree to follow a number of rules that aren't imposed on other students—you must have a physical exam, insurance coverage, and a minimum grade point average, for example. Getting dressed in locker rooms, with open shower areas and toilet stalls, reduces your privacy level as well. After reviewing these facts, the U.S. Supreme Court decided it was reasonable for schools to test student athletes for drug use.

RELATED CASES

In addition to the formal opinion in the *Vernonia* case, written by Justice Antonin Scalia, Justice Ruth Bader Ginsburg wrote a separate opinion agreeing with the decision (a **concurring opinion**). In it she raised the possibility of schools requiring  routine drug testing of all students. This opens the door for future discussion and, possibly, another case for the U.S. Supreme Court to decide. For now, the debate continues, in classrooms and courtrooms across the country.

• Should students who want to participate in any extracurricular activity be forced to undergo drug tests?

In Oklahoma, the Tecumseh Independent School District passed a policy requiring all middle school and high school students participating in extracurricular activities to submit to random drug testing. Lindsay Earls was a student at Tecumseh and a member of the choir, marching band, Academic Team, and National Honor Society. Lindsay tested negative for drug use, but found the test humiliating and accusatory. She and her parents filed a lawsuit challenging the policy. In 2002, the U.S. Supreme Court upheld the policy, stating that it was not a significant invasion of a student's privacy and that school districts have an "important interest in preventing and deterring drug use among its schoolchildren." The Court's five to four decision, written by Justice Clarence Thomas, greatly increased the number of students eligible for lawful drug testing in American schools.

Board of Education v. Earls (2002)

• Can schools require students who are suspended to be tested for drugs before returning to school?

Highland High School in Anderson, Indiana, required suspended students to undergo drug testing as a requirement for readmission. This policy applied to all suspended students—it didn't matter whether they were suspected of using drugs. James R. Willis was a freshman who faced a five-day suspension for fighting. The school had no evidence James had been using drugs or alcohol but still required him to be tested for drug use. He refused the test and went to court. The court agreed with James; he was allowed to return to school without taking the drug test. In 1999, the U.S. Supreme Court let this ruling stand.

Anderson Community School Corps. v. Willis (1999)

GET ON THE CASE

- Are you surprised by any of the decisions about drug tests? What's next—do you think all students, regardless of whether they're involved in clubs or activities outside of class, will be subject to random, suspicionless drug testing? Will this keep drugs off school grounds? Or will students continue using drugs and take a chance that on any given day, for example, they won't be picked for a drug test? What about testing for cigarette use? Do you think this is going too far, or is there a good reason for such a school rule?

● You may have heard about drug testing of professional and Olympic athletes. But did you know that drug tests are being required more frequently of adults in other fields? Often, such policies are being challenged in court. Review the following cases and then consider the questions below.

Firefighters: In Mesa, Arizona, the city fire department implemented a substance abuse program that required firefighters to submit to a drug test within thirty minutes of being told. The program included a suspicionless test that would be done randomly throughout the year. Firefighter Craig Petersen challenged the random testing component of the program, claiming it violated his right to privacy and it was an illegal search (one without suspicion of wrongdoing). The Arizona Supreme Court agreed and stopped the city from enforcing this part of the program. *Petersen v. City of Mesa* (2004)

School bus drivers: M. C. English worked for an Alabama school district as a mechanic who also drove school buses occasionally. In January 1995, he was fired from his job after testing positive for marijuana use. (This drug test was required under the federal Transportation Employee Testing Act of 1991.) M. C. sued the school district and lost. The federal district court found that the test was a minimal intrusion into M. C.'s privacy and was justified in order to guard the safety of children. *M. C. English v. Talledega County Board of Education* (1996)

Political candidates: In 1997, the U.S. Supreme Court declared a Georgia law requiring drug testing of all political candidates unconstitutional. The Court reviewed the recent history of drug testing in America and decided that drug tests are a search under the Fourth Amendment and must be reasonable—based on a suspicion that a person is breaking the law. People whose jobs affect public safety, such as airline pilots and railroad employees, may be required to submit to suspicionless tests. Because politicians and candidates for office don't usually perform high-risk or safety-sensitive tasks, this test was considered unlawful. *Chandler v. Miller* (1997)

Transit officers: In New Jersey, the transit (train) authority's police officers carry weapons and may use deadly force in certain circumstances. Their job includes promoting the safety of all employees and customers by creating a drug- and alcohol-free workplace. Requiring these officers to submit to random testing was found to be reasonable under the law. *New Jersey Local 304 v. New Jersey Transit* (1997)

Electrical engineers: David Rebel was an electrical engineer at a nuclear power plant in Pennsylvania. All employees were subject to random drug testing, and David was selected to test in 1995. He refused, claiming he didn't believe in the program. He considered the test to be an insult and an invasion of his privacy. David was fired and also denied unemployment benefits, on the grounds that his loss of employment was his own doing. He appealed his case and lost. The Commonwealth Court of Pennsylvania upheld the drug-testing policy. *Rebel v. Unemployment Compensation Board* (1997)

- What do you think about each of these cases? Do you agree that candidates for public office shouldn't be required to undergo drug tests? Or should all who hold office, regardless of level, be expected to live drug- and alcohol-free?

- Can you think of any jobs or activities where drug testing should *absolutely* be done? Do you believe some workers should *never* be required to take such tests? Why?

- Research the history of drug testing—at the library or online. When were drug tests first given and why? What group of people was first required to take these tests? Were such requirements immediately met with objections? Are the tests themselves always accurate?

Do you have privacy rights at school?

Case: *New Jersey v. T. L. O.* (1985)

Schools today are faced with the difficult task of protecting students in an age where violent outbursts and underage drug use seem common. Yet, as new measures are introduced to ensure the safety of students, teachers, and school personnel—metal detectors, video cameras, and security officers, to name a few—questions about students' rights to privacy invariably crop up. Likewise, as school administrators strive to enforce drug policies—which sometimes means conducting random locker and canine searches, as well as personal searches—they run the risk of sacrificing students' privacy.

Justice Byron White summed up the issue this way: "How, then, should we strike the balance between the schoolchild's legitimate expectation of privacy and the school's equally legitimate need to maintain an environment in which learning can take place?"

THE FACTS

In March 1980, Lenore Chen, a teacher at Piscataway High School in New Jersey, caught T. L. O. (Terry), who was a fourteen-year-old freshman, and another girl smoking in the bathroom. She took the two girls to the principal's office, where they were questioned by the assistant principal, Mr. Choplick. Terry's friend admitted to violating the school's no-smoking rule, but Terry denied that she'd been smoking. Mr. Choplick asked Terry for her purse, opened it, and immediately saw a pack of cigarettes. While reaching for the cigarettes, he noticed a pack of rolling papers, which he knew were usually used with marijuana. Mr. Choplick then thoroughly searched Terry's purse. He found a small amount of marijuana and a metal pipe, empty plastic bags, an index card that listed students who owed her money, two letters that suggested drug dealing, and $40, mostly in $1 bills. The school turned the matter over to the police. At the police station, in the presence of her mother, Terry confessed to selling drugs at school. She was charged with possession of marijuana and was later found guilty.

Terry **appealed** her case, claiming that Mr. Choplick had violated her Fourth Amendment protection (see the **Bill of Rights** on pages 18–19) against an unreasonable **search and seizure.** Terry's attorney argued that her confession at the police station should be disregarded because it resulted from the unlawful search of her purse.

YOU BE THE JUDGE

● Do you think the assistant principal's search of Terry's purse was legal? Why or why not? Did it violate Terry's Fourth Amendment protection against unreasonable searches?

● Do constitutional protections apply to students in public schools? Or can schools create and enforce their own set of rules?

THE RULING

In a six to three decision, written by Justice Byron White, the U.S. Supreme Court ruled that the initial search of Terry's purse for cigarettes was reasonable based on the teacher's report that she'd been smoking in the bathroom. Then, the assistant principal's discovery of the rolling papers created a reasonable suspicion that Terry possessed marijuana, which justified further exploration. Terry was sentenced to one year of **probation** and ordered to receive counseling and to enter a drug program.

T. L. O. is the landmark case on the issue of search and seizure at school. In this case, the Court needed to determine how to balance a student's right to privacy and the school's need to maintain an environment of learning. The Court decided that a "reasonableness" test could settle such questions.

First, it's clear that you're protected against unreasonable searches at school—your constitutional rights aren't left behind once you "enter the schoolhouse." As a student, you have a reasonable expectation of privacy that's balanced with the school's duty to do its job—to ensure the security and safety of students, to maintain order, and to promote an environment where education thrives.

The rules of this case apply only to public schools, not private and parochial schools. Because public schools receive government money, school officials are viewed as acting on behalf of the government and must follow the rules of the Constitution. People who work in private schools, on the other hand, aren't viewed as government employees and may conduct searches whenever they see fit.

This means school officials may search you and your property if they have a "reasonable suspicion" that you've broken a school rule or have committed, or are in the process of committing, a crime. The U.S. Supreme Court said the decision to search a student must be based on the "totality of circumstances"—including the student's age, history, and school records; the seriousness of the problem in the school (for example, weapons, drugs, or stolen property); and the source of information. These are called "suspicion-based" searches. There are also "suspicionless searches," in which everyone in a certain group or classification is subject to a search.

In order for a suspicion-based search to be legal, it must be justified at the beginning—reasonable grounds must exist to believe that the search will turn up evidence that a person violated a rule or law. The search must also be conducted within reasonable limits. The age and gender of the student must be considered, as well as the importance of the object of the search.

RELATED CASES

The *T. L. O.* case didn't ultimately settle what protection the Fourth Amendment offers students. Since this U.S. Supreme Court decision, courts around the country have reviewed hundreds of cases involving student searches. The increase of weapons and drugs in schools has become a "compelling circumstance" justifying more searches. However, the issue of reasonableness isn't always clear. Courts have accepted some searches as reasonable under certain circumstances, while deeming similar ones as unreasonable.

• Can school officials legally search you based on what other students report?

At Ingraham High School in Seattle, Washington, a security officer stopped two students, Eric and Adrian, who were entering the school after classes had begun. Both smelled of marijuana and had red, droopy eyes. They were questioned separately, and each admitted that he'd smoked marijuana with another student, John Washington, that morning before school. A marijuana pipe was found in their possession, but no marijuana. The security officer knew that John Washington had been involved in a previous drug-related incident. John was taken out of his gym class and escorted to the principal's office. The officer searched John, who at first protested but later consented when told the police would be called. The officer found a plastic bag containing twelve pieces of crack cocaine in John's shirt pocket. John was charged with drug possession and found guilty. He challenged the search, claiming it was illegal. The Washington Court of Appeals ruled that the amount of suspicion against John justified the warrantless search by the school official. *State v. Washington* (1999)

• Can school officials decide to search the entire student body?

Jane Doe (not her real name) was in seventh grade when she and her classmates were ordered to empty their pockets and place their backpacks and purses on their desks. While they waited in the hall, all of their belongings were searched. A container with marijuana was found in Jane's purse. Jane challenged the school's policy of random, suspicionless searches. The court agreed with Jane and recognized that students have a limited expectation of privacy at school. More than a mere apprehension of the existence of drugs or weapons is needed to justify a broad random search.

Jane plead guilty to a **misdemeanor** drug possession and was placed on probation to include a curfew and drug screens. *Jane Doe v. Little Rock School District* (2004)

• If they suspect you of wrongdoing, can school officials search your belongings?

Ninth-grader James DesRoches attended Granby High School in Norfolk, Virginia. He took an art class that met before and after lunch. In May 1997, his classmate Shamra Hursey went to lunch, leaving her tennis shoes on top of her desk. When she returned, her shoes were gone. The dean ordered a search of the belongings of the nineteen students in the class. James wouldn't let school personnel search his backpack, so he was sent to the principal's office. He called his parents and continued to refuse the search. James was suspended for ten days. He and his father sued the principal, the school superintendent, and the school board. They claimed the search would violate James's protection against unreasonable searches. The federal court who heard the case upheld the school suspension. It stated that, although James wasn't a suspect at the beginning of the incident, he became one after the other eighteen students were searched and nothing was found. By the process of elimination, James became a suspect in the question of the missing shoes, which justified a search of his backpack.

DesRoches v. Caprio (1998)

Is it reasonable for students to expect their schoolwork and grades to be kept private? The answer is no. In 2002, the U.S. Supreme Court ruled that grading each other's tests and reading the scores out loud in class does not violate a student's privacy. *Owasso v. Falvo* (2002)

• Do school officials have the right to search you during classes that are held off campus?

Seventeen-year-old Jason, a high school student in Apple Valley, Minnesota, participated in an auto-shop class. The class was on its way to a car repair shop in a neighboring city when Jason's teacher, who was driving the school bus, saw Jason with a knife in his hand. Jason and his classmates were searched by the school liaison officer. A nine-inch metal baton was found in Jason's front pocket. Jason was charged with possession of a dangerous weapon on school property. His case was **diverted** from court and he served a six-month probation period. Meanwhile, the school started expulsion proceedings against Jason for violating its ban on weapons; this resulted in a short suspension period. Jason filed a civil lawsuit in federal court against the liaison officer and the city for allegedly violating his right to be free from an unreasonable search and seizure. Under the school's no-weapons policy, the court said the search was reasonable and justified. Since the students were involved in a school function and under the supervision of their teacher, the school rules applied even off campus.

Shade v. City of Farmington (2002)

• What if you're off school grounds and not at a school-related function? Can school resource officers still search you?

At Alhambra High School in Phoenix, Arizona, a school security officer saw a student at a market across the street from the school.

He had been told the student was showing a gun to other kids. The security officer went over to the area and asked the juvenile identified as Roy if he had a gun. He said he did and was patted down. A six-shot revolver was found in his pocket. Roy was charged with and convicted of carrying a concealed weapon. Roy appealed this decision, arguing that he shouldn't have been stopped or searched. The appeals court held that the stop, search, and charge were valid. Roy was sent to the department of juvenile corrections.

In re Roy L. (2000)

• Does an "alert" by a drug-sniffing dog justify a locker search?

At Harborcreek High School in Erie County, Pennsylvania, an unannounced canine search of all 2,000 student lockers was conducted. Rudy, the dog, "hit" on eighteen of the lockers, which were then opened and searched. Marijuana and drug paraphernalia were found in a student named Vincent's jacket, which was hanging in his locker. Vincent admitted the marijuana and related items were his but argued the search was conducted illegally. The school contended the purpose of the search was to maintain a drug-free campus and was therefore legal. The Superior Court of Pennsylvania disagreed with the school, ruling that the alert by a drug-trained dog alone didn't justify a locker search. The court said Vincent had a reasonable expectation of privacy in his locker. Because the school had no evidence Vincent was using or dealing drugs, reasonable suspicion of illegal activity didn't exist. The charges were dropped because the results of the search couldn't be used as evidence against him.

Commonwealth v. Cass (1995)

• Is a strip-search acceptable if a drug-sniffing dog calls an "alert" to a student?

Diane Doe (not her real last name) was thirteen years old when a school-wide drug inspection at Highland Junior High in Indiana was performed. All 2,700 students were sniffed by police dogs. Depending on the dogs' behavior, some students had their pockets searched for drugs; others were told to remove their clothing for a visual examination. One of the dogs reacted to Diane, who was told to empty her pockets. She was also instructed to undress, which she did in front of two women in the nurse's office. Nothing was found. Diane and her parents sued the school district, the principal, the police chief, and the dog trainer for violating Diane's civil rights by conducting the search. The federal court agreed with Diane and her parents that the search was unreasonable, stating: "[I]t does not require a constitutional scholar to conclude that a nude search of a thirteen-year-old child is an invasion of some magnitude. More than that: it is a violation of any known principle of human decency."

Doe v. Renfrow (1980)

• Does a police officer's hunch justify a search?

Sixteen-year-old Demond, a student in Illinois, arrived at school one morning to discover police officers and a metal detector. Students were lined up to go through the detector. Demond turned around to leave but was stopped by the police and told to proceed through the detector. In response, Demond raised his shirt and said, "Someone put this gun on me." He was arrested and charged with possession of a weapon at school. Demond argued the search was illegal.

The Illinois Court of Appeals found that Demond's act of turning around and leaving didn't create reasonable suspicion that he possessed anything illegal. A "hunch" isn't enough to justify a search, according to the court. The police were wrong to stop Demond, so the gun was ruled as inadmissible evidence. The case against Demond was dismissed.

People v. Parker (1996)

• Is a strip-search unreasonable if the school is searching for something of little value?

After gym class in West Jay County Middle School in Dunkirk, Indiana, two seventh-grade students told their teacher that $4.50 was missing from the locker room. The principal was notified and decided to search the girls in the gym class and their lockers. Thirteen-year-old Amanda and five of her friends were interviewed by the principal. The girls were then told to take off their shoes and socks; their lockers and book bags were also searched. Then, in front of a female school official, they were told to loosen or remove their bras and shirts. Amanda, her five friends, and their parents all filed a lawsuit after this incident. Based on the object of the search ($4.50), the court ruled that a strip-search was unreasonable.

Oliver v. McClung (1995)

GET ON THE CASE

● How much authority should school officials have over you while you're at school? Where do you draw the line, and based on what—age, gender, the extent of the search?

● Considering recent incidents of school violence in the United States, what do you think schools could do to provide a safer environment for learning? Put yourself in the shoes of a teacher or principal—is your opinion on these issues the same from this standpoint? Why or why not?

● What rules or policies does your school have on searches of lockers or students? Check your student handbook or ask your principal for a copy of this written policy. Then talk to other students and your parents about the policy. Do you agree or disagree with it? Why? How do you think the policy works or doesn't work? How would you change or improve it if you could?

ISSUE:

Do you have to wait until you're eighteen to get some privacy?

Case: *Tariq A-R Y v. Maryland* (1998)

As you grow older, it's only natural to want some privacy. After all, you can't become an adult if you don't break away from your parents and develop thoughts and dreams all your own. And all of these changes require space and time to yourself.

While everyone needs privacy, a person's legal right to this freedom isn't always clear. Different people, and different courts, have varying views on what parts of your life deserve to be kept private—and what age you need to be to have privacy rights.

THE FACTS

In May 1995, an anonymous tip sent the police to Tariq's home in Frederick County, Maryland. Tariq was a **minor** who lived with his mother. When he answered the door, the police officers saw a bottle of beer on the floor and smelled marijuana in the air and alcohol on Tariq's breath.

Suspecting that Tariq was drinking alcohol or using illegal drugs, the police officers asked his mother for permission to search the home. She said yes, they could search the house and "anything in it." The officers found a bag of marijuana in a vest that was in the dining room. Tariq admitted the vest belonged to him but argued that, without his permission, the police had no right to search it.

Tariq was arrested for possession of an illegal substance. He punched and kicked the officers when he was arrested, so he was also charged with resisting arrest.

YOU BE THE JUDGE

- Can a parent of a minor give police permission to search a child's personal belongings—over the child's objection?

- The Fourth Amendment (see the **Bill of Rights** on pages 18–19) protects each of us from unreasonable **search and seizure.** This right may be **waived** by the person being searched. The question in this case is who may waive this right—the minor or the minor's parent?

- Tariq didn't expect the police to search his vest; he assumed that his privacy would be recognized and honored. Was Tariq's expectation reasonable?

Legally, you're considered a minor, juvenile, or child until you're eighteen. Then you're emancipated (free) and recognized as an adult. Once you're emancipated, your parents or legal **guardians** are no longer responsible for you or your actions. They now have no authority over you, and you no longer have the right to be taken care of by them except under special circumstances (for example, if you attend college or have certain disabilities).

You automatically become emancipated when you turn eighteen. Some states, however, allow teenagers to **petition** the courts for **emancipation** before they're eighteen, under special circumstances. The case of *Rachel Kingsley v. Gregory Kingsley* (1993) on pages 30–33 explores this issue in more depth.

THE RULING

The Maryland Court of Appeals stood by the principle that parents have the authority to make decisions about their homes and everything in them. The state court also reviewed the concept of reasonable expectation of privacy and concluded it
wasn't reasonable for Tariq to expect his belongings left in an open area of his mother's home to be viewed as private. After considering the circumstances of the search, the court ruled that the police didn't need Tariq's permission to search his property: his mother's consent was enough, and Tariq's objection didn't matter.

Reasonable is a key word when it comes to privacy and the law. Courts recognize that everyone needs and deserves a certain amount of privacy—what they call a "reasonable expectation of privacy." But what's reasonable to one person may not be to another.

Tariq was convicted of possession of marijuana and resisting arrest. His case was **appealed** to the U.S. Supreme Court, which turned down the request to hear the case in 1998. The Maryland ruling stayed in place. Tariq was sent to Maryland's department of juvenile services.

This case demonstrates that, legally, parents have authority over their underage children. Besides being in charge of the home, your parents can legally control and make decisions about where you go to school, what place of worship you attend, whether you can get a job, what sports you're allowed to play, and whom you can spend your free time with. Does this mean your parents have control over *every* aspect of your life? No, some parts *are* beyond their control. See *Bellotti v. Baird* (1979) on pages 92–96 and *Parham v. J. R.* (1979) on pages 147–151 for more information.

The law doesn't specifically give minors the right to privacy in their parents' homes. Rather, the law views privacy as a family matter—an issue individual teens and their parents should discuss and decide for themselves.

RELATED CASES

Courts continue to wrestle with the notion of privacy as it applies to adults and teenagers. Although the Fourth Amendment guards you against unreasonable personal searches and property seizures, this isn't an absolute protection. Depending on the  circumstances, you and your property may be subject to a search— at home, in a car, at school, on the Internet, or even in your trash!

• Do you have to identify yourself to the police when asked?

Larry Hiibel was standing next to his truck in Humboldt County, Nevada, when the police pulled up. A caller reported seeing a man assault a woman in a red and silver truck. A young woman was sitting inside Larry's truck. When the officer asked Larry for some identification, he refused, saying he had done nothing wrong. After being asked for his ID eleven times, Larry was arrested and charged with obstructing a police officer in carrying out his duty to investigate a reported offense. Larry was convicted and fined $250. He appealed, arguing that Nevada's "stop and identify"' statute violated his Fourth and Fifth Amendment rights—that asking for ID was an illegal search and being forced to answer violated his right against self-incrimination. The U.S. Supreme Court upheld the conviction, stating that a police officer is free to ask a person for identification. The Court said, "[A]sking questions is an essential part of police investigations."

Hiibel v. Sixth Judicial District Court of Nevada (2004)

• Can a parent record a child's telephone conversations without the child's consent?

G. was fourteen years old when her telephone conversations with a thirty-five-year-old man were recorded by her mother. Her mother became suspicious about what was going on with her daughter after reading passages in G.'s diary. Because the conversations were sexually explicit, the man was charged and convicted of various sex offenses. He appealed, arguing (among other things) that the conversations were recorded illegally. The Arizona court ruled that as long as a parent or guardian has a good faith, objectively reasonable basis for believing it is necessary and in the best interests of the minor, the parent may record a child's telephone conversations.

State v. Morrison (2002)

"We cannot attribute to Congress the intent to subject parents to criminal and civil penalties for recording their minor child's phone conversations out of concern for the child's well-being."—*Scheib v. Grant* (1994)

• Can the police search you, without a warrant, on an anonymous tip that you're carrying a weapon?

In 1995, the police in Miami, Florida, received an anonymous tip that a young black male was carrying a gun. The informant said the young man was at a bus stop with two other kids and was wearing a plaid shirt. Within minutes, the police were at the bus stop, where they saw J. L. and two boys. Fifteen-year-old J. L. did have on a plaid shirt, but he wasn't acting suspicious or making any threatening movements. The police didn't see a firearm as they approached the boys at the bus stop. Without asking any questions, one officer ordered J. L. to put his hands up; the officer then frisked him, finding a gun in the young man's pocket. J. L. was arrested and charged with possessing and carrying a concealed weapon. He argued the search was illegal and the evidence (the gun) shouldn't be used against him. The U.S. Supreme Court agreed in a unanimous decision in March 2000. Justice Ruth Bader Ginsburg wrote that the reasonableness of a police officer's suspicion must be measured by what was known *before* the search took place. An unreliable anonymous tip isn't enough to stop and frisk an individual for suspicion of criminal activity.

Florida v. J. L. (2000)

• Can the police legally search your belongings if you're not a criminal suspect?

Billie Joe Lowrimore and her mother were arguing at home in Seattle, Washington, when Billie threatened to kill herself. Her parents called the police and told them about Billie's threat and that she possessed knives. Upon arrival, police officers searched Billie's bag and purse. They found three knives, some drug-related items, and a plastic bag containing illegal drugs. Billie was put into **detention** for a seventy-two-hour mental health evaluation and treatment; she was also arrested for drug possession. Billie challenged her detention and the search of her bag and purse, which had been conducted without a **warrant.**

This case raises the issue of **criminal** versus **civil detention.** Although she ended up being charged with a crime, Billie's detention was unrelated to her criminal case. Rather, she was detained to protect herself and others from possible harm (a civil detention). The Washington State Court of Appeals ruled that such a detention is justified if a person poses a danger to self or others. A search in connection with a civil detention is for the protection of the individual detained and for the safety of the police. In situations where time is critical, a warrantless search is legal. Therefore, the court ruled that the search of Billie's bag and purse was appropriate.

State v. Lowrimore (1992)

• If your behavior is suspicious, can police legally enter your private property and conduct a search without a warrant or your consent?

Bounmy V., a minor, was spotted by the police in the driver's seat of a car parked in his carport in Modesto, California. He and three of his friends were flashing the car's lights and whistling to passing vehicles. Suspecting the friends were selling drugs from the car, the police approached the vehicle and ordered the teens to get out while they searched it. The officers discovered four pieces of rock cocaine under the backseat.

Bounmy failed to convince the court that the warrantless search of his car was illegal. The California Court of Appeals ruled that the observed activity, taking place in an open area, reduced his **zone and expectation of privacy.**

In re Bounmy V. (1993)

• What if your behavior is not suspicious? Can police still search your car?

One night at the University of Maine in Bangor, police approached the parked car of a student named Joshua and told him to roll down his window. The police had not seen any illegal behavior when they made this request. Instead of rolling down his window, Joshua opened his door and the officer smelled alcohol and cigarette smoke. Joshua was charged with operating a vehicle while under the influence of alcohol. The trial court granted Joshua's motion to suppress any evidence seized after the officer approached his car, because there was no reasonable suspicion of criminal activity and because Joshua had a reasonable expectation of privacy while in his car. The state appealed the trial court's decision to exclude the evidence and lost. This was ruled a seizure without reasonable suspicion. Other courts have come to different conclusions on similar searches.

State v. Patterson (2005)

• Is your property private when you're a passenger in a vehicle?

In 1999, the U.S. Supreme Court made a decision that reduced a person's zone of privacy. In this case, Sandra Houghton, a legal adult in Wyoming, was riding in a car stopped for speeding. The driver had a syringe in his shirt pocket and, when asked, admitted he'd used it to take drugs. Sandra lied about her name, had fresh needle tracks on her arms, and, when the car was searched, told the police the purse on the backseat was hers. During the search, the police found methamphetamine and drug-related items in Sandra's purse. She was arrested and later convicted of drug possession and

sentenced to two to three years in prison. On appeal, the search of Sandra's purse was upheld by the U.S. Supreme Court. The justices determined that, when you are a passenger in a car, your expectation of privacy is considerably less than in other situations.
Wyoming v. Houghton (1999)

• Is your garbage private property?

In July 1992, sanitation worker Nelson Dowd picked up Allen Hauser's garbage as he did every week in Winston-Salem, North Carolina. This time, though, at the direction of the police, Nelson kept it separate from the rest of the trash. (Note: a private citizen wouldn't normally be given such a task, except at the request of the police.) He turned the garbage over to the authorities, who found evidence of cocaine possession. Allen was convicted and sentenced to ten years in prison. He appealed, claiming the search and seizure of his garbage was illegal. The North Carolina Appeals Court disagreed, holding that any expectation of privacy was lost once the garbage was put out for the public to see and take. This case demonstrates that, regardless of age, a person's right to privacy is limited.
State v. Hauser (1995)

• Can adults other than your parents give police permission to search your property?

Dion Summers and a friend were seen walking down the street carrying stereo equipment. A burglary had been reported earlier that day in Dion's neighborhood in Seattle, Washington. His mother was out of town, and Dion's adult sister was staying at the house, caring for the children. She later gave the police permission to search Dion's room, where the stereos were found. Dion was charged with and convicted of burglary. He argued that his sister didn't have the authority to allow a search of his belongings. The Washington State Court of Appeals disagreed, ruling that his sister, who was in charge of the minor during his mother's absence, did indeed possess this authority.
State v. Summers (1988)

• When is an "expectation of privacy" considered reasonable?

In Bend, Oregon, nineteen-year-old Eugene Carsey was on parole and was required to live with his grandparents. He paid them $60 a month to rent a room in their home. His grandparents never entered his room, based on an unspoken agreement that he alone had control over it. He cleaned it himself and did his own laundry. On a tip that Eugene had received stolen stereo equipment, the police conducted a warrantless search of his room and found marijuana. Although Eugene's grandmother had given her permission to search his room, in this case, the state court determined that her consent was invalid. Under the family's living arrangements, Eugene had a reasonable expectation of privacy.

State v. Carsey (1983)

GET ON THE CASE

● Do you think everyone deserves privacy? Under what circumstances should a person's right to privacy be taken away? Is it important to you to keep some of your belongings and thoughts private? Why?

● What about when someone keeps a journal? Do you think this should always be kept private, or are there certain circumstances when it should be allowed as court evidence? Why? What about personal mail or email? How private should these items be in the eyes of the law?

● Hold a family meeting to discuss the issue of privacy. Talk about how family members can respect each other's privacy and what is and isn't private in your home.

ISSUE:

Can you be tried as an adult and receive an adult sentence?

Case: *Kent v. United States* (1966)

Although juvenile courts were created to decide cases against **minors,** more and more often teenagers are being tried in adult court. A move into adult court means juveniles may receive longer sentences for their crimes—instead of being released when they turn eighteen or twenty-one. Their sentence is also focused on punishment and protecting the community, rather than rehabilitation and treatment—the goals of juvenile court.

THE FACTS

Morris Allen Kent was arrested in Washington, D.C., on September 5, 1961, for three home burglaries, three robberies, and two counts of rape. The sixteen-year-old had been on **probation** since he was fourteen for burglary and purse snatching.

Morris was held in **detention** for almost a week. (At the time of Morris's arrest, the District of Columbia allowed minors to be held for up to five days before a hearing—now it's a maximum of forty-eight hours.) His mother hired a lawyer who arranged for two psychiatrists and a psychologist to evaluate Morris to determine his mental state. Morris's lawyer wanted to argue that Morris's case should be kept in the juvenile court—not go into adult court. His lawyer asked the juvenile court for a hearing on the question of **waiver** to adult court, and he asked for Morris's **social file,** so he could be better informed about his client's history. The psychiatrist found Morris to be "a victim of severe psychopathology" and recommended hospitalization.

The court didn't respond to these requests or to the psychiatrist's evaluation. No hearing was held, and neither Morris, his parents, nor an attorney were allowed to address the court. The court signed a waiver "after full investigation" that sent Morris to adult court. No reasons for the waiver were given. The jury found Morris guilty of the burglary and robbery charges, but not guilty by reason of insanity of the rape charges. The court sentenced Morris to thirty to ninety years in prison.

Morris and his attorney **appealed,** arguing that the court wasn't given enough information about Morris's mental state or his history. They said he shouldn't have been charged or tried in adult court.

YOU BE THE JUDGE

- Do you think Morris should have been waived into adult court under these circumstances? Why or why not?

- What factors do you think the court considers when deciding whether to waive a minor into adult court?

THE RULING

This is a key case in the law of juvenile rights. Because the U.S. Supreme Court thought some of the police and juvenile court practices were "disturbing," it examined the juvenile court system for the first time. In particular, it looked at **due process** and fair treatment of juveniles before **transfer** to adult court.

The Court determined that waiving a minor into adult court is a "critically important" issue that requires fair treatment, a thorough investigation, and careful consideration. Courts need to follow the laws of their individual states when making the waiver decision. These state laws outline the factors courts need to consider, including the seriousness of the crime; how it was committed; the juvenile's age, maturity, and lifestyle; whether the offense is a personal or property crime; and the minor's criminal background and mental state. Community safety is to be considered, as well as the likelihood of rehabilitating the juvenile in the juvenile justice system.

The Court felt strongly about protecting an individual's rights when faced with a criminal charge. It recognized the consequences of sending a juvenile to adult court and wanted to create strict safeguards in the process. In a five to four decision, Justice Abe Fortas wrote: "There is no place in our system of law for reaching a result of such tremendous consequences without ceremony—without hearing, without effective assistance of counsel, without a statement of reasons." The Court ruled that a hearing must be held to decide whether to transfer a juvenile into adult court, the juvenile must be given an opportunity to address the court with the assistance of an attorney, and the court must provide an explanation of its decision.

Courts generally recognize that juveniles lack the experience, judgment, and maturity of adults. Consequently, they are seen as good candidates for rehabilitation. Rehabilitation may include probation, community service, a fine, **restitution** to victims, individual and family counseling, and detention. The majority of juveniles who successfully complete a juvenile court sentence have no further contact with the justice system.

The Court found that the lower court violated Morris's rights. The case was sent back to the trial court to determine whether Morris should be transferred into adult court. The federal district court considered the U.S. Supreme Court's position on Morris's rights but again decided that Morris should be tried as an adult. Another court of appeals later reversed this decision, due to Morris's mental condition. It found Morris was mentally ill and needed psychiatric treatment, not prison. The court set aside the conviction and sentence, and ordered Morris to remain hospitalized under the **civil commitment laws.**

An 1843 English case that became known as the M'Naghten Rule of Insanity established the test that a number of states use today in criminal trials. It states a person isn't criminally responsible for his or her crime if, at the time of committing the act, the person didn't know (1) what he or she was doing and (2) that the act was wrong and violated the rights of another. Those states that don't use M'Naghten have their own test for determining criminal responsibility.

Although the *Kent* decision is forty years old, its principle is continually turned to—that juveniles can be treated as adults in the criminal system, but they must be afforded full due process throughout the proceedings. It's a serious matter for teenagers to face adult consequences for their acts. The responsibility for deciding a teenager's fate weighs heavily on all of the participants.

RELATED CASES

In some states, juveniles charged with certain crimes start off in adult court—the juvenile must convince the court he or she belongs in juvenile court instead. Arkansas, New York, Oklahoma, and Vermont are some states that proceed in this manner. It's a legislative decision, based in part on community protection. Other states have a direct-file policy regarding certain crimes. If the juvenile is a certain age and allegedly commits a specific offense (usually a violent crime), the charges are filed in adult court and *stay* there. Arizona, Florida, Kansas, and Massachusetts are four states with a direct-file procedure.

• Can you receive a sentence for juvenile detention *and* prison?

J. W. was thirteen years old when she moved from her grand-mother's home to live with her mother in Schaumburg, Illinois. On her first day there she wrote in her diary about killing her mother with a knife. J. W. felt her mother loved her live-in boyfriend more than she loved J. W. A few days later J. W. attacked her mother with three knives. After a few days in the hospital, her mother died. She had suffered over 200 cuts, punctures, and stab wounds. J. W. confessed and was found guilty of first-degree murder. Under Illinois **extended jurisdiction law,** J. W. was sentenced to five years in juvenile detention and thirty-five years in prison once she turned eighteen—this is called a *blended sentence* because it crosses over from one jurisdiction (juvenile) to another (adult) upon reaching a certain age. J. W. appealed this sentence, arguing it was excessive given her age, her lack of a previous criminal record, and the time she had remaining in the juvenile justice system to be rehabilitated. The Appellate Court of Illinois disagreed, stating that under the circumstances of this case, J. W.'s sentence was not excessive.
In re J. W. (2004)

• Can you be tried as an adult if you're only eleven years old?

In 1997, eleven-year-old Nathaniel Abraham borrowed a rifle and randomly shot and killed eighteen-year-old Ronnie Greene Jr. in Pontiac, Michigan. Nathaniel was 70 yards away from Ronnie, who was standing outside a convenience store when the shooting took place. Under Michigan law, Nathaniel was tried as an adult and convicted in 1999 of second-degree murder. Michigan law allowed the court to sentence him either as a juvenile or an adult, or under a blended sentence that would require him to be under supervision past the age of twenty-one. The judge stated that although Nathaniel committed a heinous crime, there were eight years left to rehabilitate him; the judge preferred this option over sending the boy to an adult prison, where rehabilitation and treatment wouldn't be available. In January 2000, Nathaniel was sentenced to a juvenile detention facility until the age of twenty-one. At this point, he had already been locked up for two years, and the judge noticed Nathaniel had made progress during that time.

In re Abraham (1999)

• How does the type of crime influence whether a minor will be tried in adult court?

In a case in Iowa, Mario Terry (age sixteen), his girlfriend Jessica Springsteen (fifteen), and another boy, Thomas Hull, went to Harold Mitchell's home, where they beat him with a baseball bat and a crowbar. Mr. Mitchell was Jessica's stepfather, who disapproved of Jessica and Mario's relationship and had banned Mario from his home. The man survived the beating, with minor back injuries. Under Iowa law, juveniles charged with certain crimes start in adult court and argue to be moved to juvenile court. Mario and his lawyers were unable to persuade the state trial court that he should be treated as a juvenile rather than an adult. The age of all three teens, their motivation, and the circumstances of the crime along with all legal requirements were considered in deciding whether to change the **jurisdiction** of Mario's case. A jury convicted him of attempted murder and first-degree burglary (entering the house with the intent to commit a crime). He was sentenced to twenty-five years in prison.

State v. Terry (1997)

In most states, minors don't have a fundamental right to be prosecuted as juveniles. Instead, it's considered a privilege granted by the legislature. This means each state may set its own age and other guidelines for which cases go to juvenile court and which ones fall under the jurisdiction of an adult court—as long as the state laws don't treat people in the same class differently. For example, in 1995, Wisconsin lowered the age for adult prosecution to ten for juveniles charged with murder. This applies to all ten-year-olds, whether boys or girls.

• Do minors have a right to have their parents with them in court?

School was just getting out at Miller Grove Middle School in Georgia. Behind one of the buildings, fourteen-year-old Fabian Appling approached two boys and, at gunpoint, took the shoes and wallet of one of the boys. Fabian was charged with armed robbery and was tried as an adult. During the trial, the prosecution excluded witnesses from the courtroom—all witnesses who were to testify had to stay out of the courtroom until it was their turn to take the stand. (This is done to prevent witnesses from hearing the testimony of others and possibly changing their story; it's a common practice in criminal trials.) In this case, Fabian's mother was listed as a possible witness, because she may have noticed her son's behavior after the incident and heard statements he made about the robbery.

Fabian was found guilty. He and his lawyer appealed the conviction, arguing that his mother should have been allowed in the courtroom to help him understand the trial and make decisions along with his lawyer. The Georgia Court of Appeals decided that a parent's right to be present at trial is not absolute. It did state, however, that trying a juvenile as an adult doesn't *make* a juvenile an adult and said: "Parental guidance in a **felony** case is a necessary safeguard for a juvenile." In this case, though, no error was found and Fabian's conviction was affirmed.

Appling v. State (1996)

Since the 1980s, the number of teenagers tried in adult court has been increasing—due to a new focus on community protection and a move away from treatment and rehabilitation of juveniles. Many states passed laws authorizing automatic waiver to adult court for certain crimes. This means, depending on the offense and age of the offender, a juvenile bypasses juvenile court and goes straight to adult court. Prosecutors have been given greater discretion in charging juvenile offenders. Those who don't go directly to adult court may still end up there through the waiver process in juvenile court. The juvenile court judge may decide the juvenile isn't appropriate for juvenile court services and the community needs protection from this individual. In such a case, the juvenile court may waive, or give up, its jurisdiction and send the case to adult court. A hearing is conducted to determine the appropriateness of treating a minor as an adult.

GET ON THE CASE

- What do you think about the factors that are considered when deciding whether to waive a minor into adult court—more specifically, the crime and how it was committed; the juvenile's age, maturity, and lifestyle; whether the offense is a personal or property crime; and the minor's criminal background and mental state? What other factors do you think the court should consider?

- What do you think about rehabilitating juveniles? Do you think most minors who get in trouble with the law can be helped? Why or why not? What do you think it would take to rehabilitate someone?

- What's the law in your state about sending juveniles to adult court? Call or write a local lawyer and ask. The police or your district attorney also may be of help; so may your local and state bar associations. The telephone numbers you need should be in the phone book or on the Internet. You can check the Yellow Pages under Attorneys or Criminal Law for the names of practicing attorneys to contact.

- Identify a local story where a juvenile has been charged with a crime and a waiver hearing is scheduled. Follow it through to the end and see if you agree with the outcome. Keep an open mind until you consider all the facts—from everyone involved, including the juvenile's witnesses as well as the victim's. Call the prosecutor and defense attorney involved with the case; explain that you're studying the process. Ask if you may follow the case to its conclusion. You may even be able to attend court as an observer. (Courts often allow observers from high schools and colleges.) Remember to ask about any confidentiality rules you may be expected to follow. Look under Attorneys or in the government section of the phone book under City Attorney, District Attorney, or Public Defender.

Can you get an abortion without a parent's consent?

Case: *Bellotti v. Baird* (1979)

If you ever broke a bone when you were little, your mom or dad probably brought you to the hospital to have a cast put on. Or if you needed surgery to have your appendix or tonsils removed, a parent was most likely by your side. Legally, your mom or dad needed to give the hospital permission to treat you.

What happens when you're older, but not yet an adult, and you want to see a doctor for something you consider private, such as birth control or an abortion? Does a parent still have to give consent for you to receive medication or have surgery?

THE FACTS

Sixteen-year-old Mary Moe was an unmarried teenager, living with her parents in Massachusetts. In October 1974, she discovered that she was eight weeks pregnant. She no longer saw the father of the baby, a sixteen-year-old boy she had dated for three months. Mary decided to have an abortion. However, in Massachusetts it was illegal for a doctor to perform an abortion on an unmarried **minor** without informing and getting the permission of both parents. If the minor's parents refused to consent, then the minor could ask a court to grant permission for the abortion. Either way, parental notice was required.

Mary didn't want to tell her parents she was pregnant. Her father had become quite upset at an earlier time when he learned that one of her friends was pregnant. Mary remembered he had said that if she got pregnant, he would kick her out of the house and kill her boyfriend. So, out of fear of what her father might do, dread about letting her parents know she'd had sex, and a desire to spare her parents' feelings, Mary chose not to tell them about her situation. She did, however, confide in her older sister.

In October 1974, Mary and the Parents Aid Society, a nonprofit clinic in Boston that performed abortions, filed a lawsuit challenging the Massachusetts law that prevented underage women from getting abortions without their parents' consent. They argued that the law discriminated against minors—that it violated their **due process** and **equal protection** rights, as outlined in the Fourteenth Amendment (see the **Bill of Rights** on pages 18–19).

Although she was a minor, the Massachusetts court determined that Mary was of average intelligence, that she fully understood the court proceedings, and that she was competent and emotionally capable of making a decision about her pregnancy without her parents' guidance. In fact, before she became pregnant, she decided that if she was faced with such a situation, she'd seek an abortion. Mary testified in court that she contacted the clinic about an abortion "about five minutes after I found out I was pregnant."

Mary received counseling and had the abortion during a time in the lawsuit when the law was suspended. The lawsuit began in 1974 and was settled in 1979.

In 1970, Norma McCorvey, an unmarried woman who lived in Dallas, Texas, learned she was pregnant. She immediately tried to get an abortion but couldn't because of an 1854 Texas law that allowed abortion only if the woman's life was in danger as a result of the pregnancy. Norma challenged the law, claiming it violated her right to privacy. Throughout her case, she used the name Jane Roe. The U.S. Supreme Court agreed with Norma and in 1973 said that the Fourteenth Amendment's protection of liberty is broad enough to include a woman's decision whether to terminate her pregnancy. The landmark case is known as *Roe v. Wade* (1973).

YOU BE THE JUDGE

- Do parents have a right to prevent their daughter from getting an abortion?

- Do parents have a right to know their daughter is seeking an abortion?

- Do you think teenage girls are capable of making this decision without their parents' help?

THE RULING

In deciding whether a teenager can get an abortion without telling her parents or getting their permission, the U.S. Supreme Court reviewed the history of parent-child relationships in terms of government protection and intervention.

The Court recognized that deeply rooted in our nation's history and traditions is the belief that parents have a great deal of authority over their children. This is basic in the structure of our society. We place certain legal restrictions on minors to protect them and to allow them to grow up in a safe environment. These include safeguards from obscenity, employment restrictions, and due process protections when arrested or charged with a crime.

The Court also noted two considerations regarding teens and abortion:

1. A substantial number of girls under eighteen are capable of forming a valid consent; this means they're mature enough to make an intelligent, well-informed decision regarding their pregnancy, after considering the options available.

2. A mother's right to an abortion in the first trimester (first three months of pregnancy) doesn't depend on her calendar age. Teen and adult mothers alike have this right.

The question then becomes how to balance the parents' right to raise their children against the underage woman's right to get an abortion.

The eight to one Court opinion, written by Justices Lewis F. Powell and John P. Stevens, strongly recommended states to encourage unmarried pregnant teens to ask their parents for help and advice: "[T]he decision whether or not to bear a child . . . is a grave decision, and a girl of tender years, under emotional stress, may be ill-equipped to make it without mature advice and emotional support."

The Court also recognized the need to make the abortion decision quickly—there may be little time between discovering a pregnancy and the end of the first trimester. Unlike other parent-child decisions (such as marriage, driving, and employment), the abortion decision can't be postponed.

Consequently, the Court determined that the Massachusetts law was unconstitutional; a state may not require parental consent for a minor's abortion without also providing another way for an underage woman to get authorization for the abortion. In other words, a state may not give parents an absolute veto over a minor's decision to have an abortion.

A state may set up what's called a **judicial bypass procedure.** In this situation, the minor may show the court she's mature enough and well informed enough to make a decision, in consultation with her doctor and independent of her parents' wishes. If not mature enough to make a decision, she may show that the abortion is in her best interests. The Court recognized that some parents hold strong views on abortion and would obstruct their daughter's access to both an abortion and the court. Consequently, a minor may go directly to the court to receive authorization for an abortion.

Justice Byron R. White disagreed with the majority of the Court. He commented on the effect of this decision, which allows a minor to obtain an abortion without parental notice or consent: "Until now, I would have thought inconceivable a holding that the United States Constitution forbids even notice to parents when their minor child who seeks surgery objects to such notice and is able to convince a judge that the parents should be denied participation in the decision."

RELATED CASES

Although the U.S. Supreme Court has recognized your right to privacy in sexual matters, it may be in your best interests to keep an open mind and an open line of communication with your mom or dad, who could be an invaluable source of advice and support. Having the ability and the right to do something doesn't mean that you have to act. There may be a better alternative, once you're fully informed and have given the situation some thought. In reading about the teens in the following cases, consider your reaction if you were in their position.

• Does your home situation affect the parental notification requirement for abortions?

Days before her eighteenth birthday, Jane Doe (not her real name) asked a juvenile court judge in Franklin County, Ohio, for permission to have an abortion without telling her parents. Jane told the court she'd been physically abused by her parents and threatened with future abuse. Although the juvenile court denied her request, a higher court granted it. Jane's "horrible home life," the Ohio court ruled, justified concealing her pregnancy from her parents.

In re Jane Doe (1994)

• Can you get an abortion without notifying either of your parents?

In 1997, the U.S. Supreme Court decided another challenge to a parent notification law. A Parental Notice of Abortion Act had been passed in Montana in 1995; it allowed an unemancipated minor to have an abortion after one of her parents was notified. The Court had already decided that requiring notice to both parents was unconstitutional.

However, a bypass provision gave Montana minors the right to convince a court that notifying either parent wouldn't be in the minor's best interests. The Court upheld this law, ruling that if clear and convincing evidence exists that any of the following three conditions are met, notice to parents may be **waived:**

1. The minor is mature enough to decide whether to have an abortion.

2. There is evidence of a pattern of physical, sexual, or emotional abuse by one of her parents or a **guardian.**

3. Notification to the parent isn't in the minor's best interests.

Lambert v. Wicklund (1997)

• If your health is in danger, can you have an abortion without informing your parents?

While the U.S. Supreme Court has yet to rule specifically on this issue, in 2006 the Court reviewed New Hampshire's Parental Notification Prior to Abortion Act. The law allowed a physician to perform an abortion on a minor without parental notification in emergency situations to prevent the girl's death. The law did not, however, state that such action was permissible if the minor's life was not at stake but her health would be endangered by delay. The lower courts ruled that the entire New Hampshire law was unconstitutional because it did not include this health exception. Justice Sandra Day O'Connor stated in the Court's unanimous decision that "the lower courts need not have invalidated the law wholesale." By reviewing what the New Hampshire legislature intended in passing the law, the Court said a "modest remedy" may be reached rather than the "most blunt remedy of invalidating it entirely." In other words, part of the law may remain as constitutional while the defective sections cannot be enforced because they're unconstitutional. The case was sent back to the lower courts for reconsideration. The Supreme Court may be deciding more challenges to parental notification laws in the near future.

Ayotte v. Planned Parenthood of Northern New England (2006)

• Do you need to get a parent's permission before getting birth control at school?

In an attempt to prevent teen pregnancy and the spread of sexually transmitted diseases among students, the Philadelphia Board of Education developed a voluntary, in-school condom distribution and counseling program. Parents could veto their children's participation in the high school program. This meant that before a student would be given condoms, a counselor would check if the student's parent had opted out. If they had, the request would be denied. If not, and after counseling regarding abstinence and appropriate use, the condoms would be provided.

A parent group asked the court to stop the program, claiming it was illegal and infringed upon students' privacy rights. The court denied this request, stating that a condom program is a legitimate service that helps keep students healthy. The court noted that a "student's education is hindered when they drop out of school because they are pregnant, sick with venereal disease, or dying of AIDS. . . . high schools must teach wellness and fitness, and give instruction regarding the prevention of HIV and AIDS."

Parents United for Better Schools v. Philadelphia Board of Education (1997)

• Do clinics have to get parents' permission before prescribing birth control pills for minors?

A public family planning clinic in Lansing, Michigan, was sued for providing contraceptive devices and medication to minors without parental notice or consent. The clinic required minors seeking contraception to attend a two-hour "rap session" about birth control methods, the responsibilities of being sexually active, and the importance of talking to parents about sexual activity. In each case, a doctor decided whether to give the minor contraceptives. Female patients had to undergo a thorough physical examination and provide a complete medical history. The federal court of appeals found that the clinic's activities didn't interfere with the parents' constitutional rights. Furthermore, the clinic didn't have a duty to notify parents of their child's visit.

Doe v. Irwin (1980)

• Do teens have the right to have sex?

Under California law, sixteen-year-old T. A. J. was charged with **statutory rape**—having sexual intercourse with someone under the legal age limit. In this case, T. A. J.'s partner, T. P., was fourteen. The California law on consensual sex with minors set penalties ranging from **probation** to prison and fines up to $25,000. (All states have some form of this law.)

T. A. J. was found guilty by the court and placed on probation. He **appealed,** claiming an invasion of privacy—that minors, closely related in age, have a right to engage in intercourse without breaking the law. The California Court of Appeals disagreed, stating that there's no privacy right among minors to have consensual sex.

In re T. A. J. (1998)

GET ON THE CASE

● The law gives a woman the right to have an abortion, but what is the definition of a *woman?* Is it any female who becomes pregnant, or a female over the age of eighteen? Do you think a minor who becomes pregnant should have a right to choose an abortion? Why or why not? Do you think the age of the minor plays a role—for example, whether the minor is twelve or seventeen?

● What rights do you think teenagers should have concerning their own bodies? At what age should a juvenile be given more rights? Why? What about birth control? Do you think minors have the right to receive prescriptions for birth control without informing their parents? Why or why not?

● Brainstorm a list of other adult rights that minors are usually restricted from (driving, voting, getting married). Choose one of these rights, and then make a list of the pros and cons of abolishing the age requirement for it. Do the pros outweigh the cons? Why or why not?

ISSUE:

Do you have complete freedom of expression at school?

Case: *Tinker v. Des Moines Independent School District* (1969)

High school is often a time when students strive to blend in with the crowd while still being unique individuals. Do you feel comfortable doing something that sets you apart from the rest of your class or might lead to criticism? The teens in this case held strong views about war, particularly the involvement of the United States in Vietnam. They took a stand, and their case became the benchmark for future free speech issues at school.

THE FACTS

In December 1965, a group of students and parents in Des Moines, Iowa, decided to express their objection to the war in Vietnam by wearing black armbands during the holiday season. The school district, fearing the protest would create a disruption, passed a policy banning armbands at school. Students who wore one would be asked to remove it. Refusal meant suspension until they returned without it.

John Tinker was fifteen and in high school. His sister Mary Beth (age thirteen) was in junior high, while Paul (eight) and Hope (eleven) Tinker attended elementary school. All four kids, along with a friend, Chris Eckhardt (fifteen), wore the two-inch-wide black cloth armbands to school. When John, Mary Beth, and Chris refused to take the bands off, they were suspended and sent home. After the holidays, they returned to school without them.

The Tinkers sued the school district, asking the court to throw out the rule as an unconstitutional violation of their freedom of expression guaranteed in the First Amendment (see the **Bill of Rights** on pages 18–19).

YOU BE THE JUDGE

- The First Amendment provides for freedom of expression. Do schools have a right to limit a student's freedom? Why or why not?

- Do you think the type of expression affects this decision? If so, how?

THE RULING

In this case, the U.S. Supreme Court needed to balance the authority of school officials to maintain order on campus and the First Amendment rights of students, including freedom of speech and expression.

The principles of this case, which remain valid today, start with the premise that students are persons in and out of school, with fundamental rights. The Court stated, in a seven to two decision written by Justice Abe Fortas, that the classroom is a marketplace of ideas and depends on a robust exchange of ideas. Students and teachers don't "shed their constitutional rights to freedom of speech or expression at the schoolhouse gate." Consequently, the school district lost this case.

The Court stated firmly that free speech on campus is the basis of our national strength and of the independence and vigor of Americans. In fact, a student's right to expression goes beyond the classroom to the cafeteria, playing field, or anyplace else on campus. "A subject should never be excluded from the classroom merely because it is controversial," the Court wrote.

Does this mean there are no limits—that you can say or do anything while at school? Where is the line drawn?

The test is one of disturbance or disorder. As long as the act of expression doesn't greatly disrupt classwork or school activities, or invade the rights of others, it's acceptable. (This is decided by a school administrator or district policy.) There's no hard-and-fast rule that applies to every situation. Each case presents its own set of circumstances and must be dealt with accordingly.

It was decided in *Tinker* that there was no evidence of disruption at school or interference with other students' rights. The armbands were a symbolic act—a "silent, passive expression of opinion" unaccompanied by any disorder. In fact, it generated discussion on the subject outside of the classroom.

Thirty years after the *Tinker* decision, the teens who took this case to court commented on how it affected their lives: John Tinker, a systems analyst, said: "Freedoms are not likely to remain, unless we exercise them. If we expect to have a democracy, schools should be a laboratory for ideas and expression."

Mary Beth Tinker, now a nurse practitioner in Missouri, supports the political activities of students who are trying to make a positive impact on the world. "You have more power than you may realize," she said.

Continued →

Chris Eckhardt, once named the kid with the cleanest locker, was asked by the vice principal if he wanted a "busted nose" after refusing to remove the armband. Now involved with politics in Florida, Eckhardt said the *Tinker* case reinforced his belief that one person can make a difference. He said: "Practice democracy daily, and exercise your rights. Stand up not only for your rights, but also for your fellow students' rights."

The Court further stated that school officials must have "more than a mere desire to avoid discomfort and unpleasantness that always accompany an unpopular viewpoint" in order to justify the limitation of student expression. It said: "Undifferentiated fear or apprehension of disturbance is not enough to overcome the right to freedom of expression."

This case supports your right to express your opinion and to protest. That right, however, isn't without limits. Responsibilities go hand in hand with rights. This means that when you act in support of an issue, you still have to respect the rights of others. At school, for example, acts that disrupt classes or the student body may be legally restricted. Off campus, there are also limits when your actions disrupt the public or infringe on the rights of others.

RELATED CASES

The following cases demonstrate that courts differ in resolving these thorny First Amendment issues. How the "disturbance" standard is interpreted varies from case to case.

• Are you free to express yourself in writing at school?

Fifteen-year-old George was in an English honors class at Santa Teresa High School in San Jose, California. He thought of poetry as art and a medium to describe emotions instead of acting them out. He shared a poem he wrote called "Dark Poetry" with several classmates. Part of it read: "I am Dark, Destructive, and Dangerous. I slap on my face of happiness but inside I am evil! For I can be the next kid to bring guns to kill students at school. So parents watch your children cuz I'm BACK!" One of the girls felt threatened by the poem and reported the incident to her teacher. George was arrested and charged with making a criminal threat. He was found guilty and sentenced to 100 days in juvenile hall. George **appealed** and the California Supreme Court ruled that the poem and the circumstances surrounding its dissemination did not measure up to a specific and immediate criminal threat.

In re George T. (2004)

• Can you be suspended for using foul language?

About twenty years after *Tinker*, the Court considered the issue of indecent or vulgar expression on campus. During an assembly at Bethel High School in Washington State, Matthew Fraser gave a nominating speech for a friend who was running for student office. His speech was filled with "elaborate, graphic, and explicit sexual metaphors," which school officials said violated the school's disruptive conduct rule. Matthew was suspended for three days and forfeited a chance to be a speaker at that year's graduation ceremony. Matthew argued that he shouldn't be punished for expressing his views, even if he used offensive language. The Court upheld the school's decision, stating that public schools have the right to prohibit the use of vulgar and offensive terms in school.

Bethel School District v. Fraser (1986)

• Can a teacher be fired for allowing students to swear?

After twenty years of teaching, a Missouri high school teacher, Cecilia Lacks, was fired for allowing her students to use profanity in their creative writing assignments and in the performance of their plays. This violated the school's ban on profanity on campus. She appealed to the U.S. Supreme Court, which in 1999 let the lower court's decision stand.

Cecilia Lacks v. Ferguson School District (1999)

• Are physical threats unacceptable or are they a form of free expression?

Fifteen-year-old Sarah Lovell spent hours one day attempting to change her class schedule at her school in California. When she thought she was finally done, the school counselor told her she might not get into certain classes because they were overloaded. Frustrated and irritated, Sarah put her head in her hands and said, "If you don't give me this schedule change, I'm going to shoot you."

The counselor reported the incident to the assistant principal, and Sarah was suspended for three days. She and her parents filed a lawsuit against the school district, the school principal, and the assistant principal, claiming a violation of free speech. The court held that threats of physical violence aren't protected by the First Amendment, saying: "[W]idespread violence in schools throughout the Nation significantly interferes with the quality of education." Sarah lost her case; her statements weren't protected by the First Amendment.

Lovell v. Poway Unified School District (1996)

• Can you circulate a petition at school?

Amanda was nine years old and in the third grade at Lackawanna Trail Elementary School in Factoryville, Pennsylvania. Her class was scheduled to take a field trip to the circus. Amanda believed the circus was cruel to animals and handwrote a petition stating, "We 3rd grade kids don't want to go to the circus because they hurt animals. We want a better field trip." She brought the petition to school and persuaded over 130 students to sign it. The next day at recess she was told to put the petition away because the playground was icy and students could get hurt if they slipped and fell while holding a pen. She was allowed to pass out coloring books and stickers addressing cruelty to animals at the circus. On the day of the circus, Amanda and her mother stood outside the gates and protested. Amanda and her parents sued the school for making her put the petition away, which they said violated her right to freedom of speech. Her case was dismissed because her actions at school were only regulated not prohibited. The court used the principles of *Tinker v. Des Moines* in deciding this case.

Walker-Serrano v. Leonard (2003)

• Can schools suspend you for wearing T-shirts with offensive language?

When Kimberly Ann Broussard was twelve years old, she bought a T-shirt at a New Kids on the Block concert. It was black with eight-inch white letters declaring "Drugs Suck!" When she wore the shirt to class at Blair Middle School in Norfolk, Virginia, it caught the attention of a teacher. She was asked to either change her shirt, turn it inside out, or borrow another shirt from a friend. Kimberly refused and was suspended for one day. Kimberly and her parents challenged this decision in court. The federal district court for Virginia ruled that, although the message against drugs was acceptable, the form wasn't. School officials may limit offensive words. *Broussard v. School Board of City of Norfolk* (1992)

• What about clothes that depict weapons? Can schools prohibit you from wearing these?

At Alan Newsom's elementary school in Virginia, the dress code prohibited any messages on clothing and jewelry that related to weapons. Alan was twelve and in the sixth grade. He wore a purple T-shirt to school that depicted three black silhouettes of men holding firearms over the letters NRA, which stand for the National Rifle Association. The graphics were described as large and bold.

Alan was asked by the assistant principal to turn his shirt inside out, which he did. From then on he wore T-shirts with the NRA letters but no graphics. He and his father sued the school board, alleging infringement of his First Amendment rights to expression. The court ruled that the dress code was overbroad and there was no evidence that messages related to weapons had caused any disruption at school or interfered with the rights of other students. *Newsom v. Albemarle County School Board* (2003)

• What if school officials think the message on your T-shirt is vulgar? Can they discipline you?

Jeffrey Pyle, a Massachusetts high school senior and band member, received three detentions for wearing offensive T-shirts to school. One of the shirts was a Christmas gift from his mother that read "Coed Naked Band—Do It to the Rhythm." Another shirt pictured a marijuana leaf and said "Legalize It."

The school dress code prohibited wearing apparel that "harassed, intimidated, or demeaned an individual because of sex, color, race, handicap, national origin, or sexual orientation." Jeff's challenge to the school policy was successful. The Massachusetts Supreme Court found that even though some of the shirts could be considered vulgar, they weren't disruptive.

Pyle v. School Commission (1996)

• Can you be suspended for your "symbolic speech"?

During lunch one day, Wayne Denno, a student in Florida, showed his friends a four-by-four-inch Confederate flag. A teacher saw the flag, told Wayne to put it away, and took him to the principal's office. Although Wayne claimed he had the flag in school because of its historical significance, he was suspended for nine days for disruptive behavior. School officials argued that Wayne attempted to start a riot, disobeyed school authorities, and encouraged another student who was wearing a T-shirt with a Confederate flag on it to stick to his principles when he was ordered to turn it inside out.

The school's actions were upheld by the federal district court in Florida, due to a history of racial tension associated with the Confederate flag. Symbolic speech (such as T-shirts, buttons, and armbands), as well as pure speech, may be restricted under certain circumstances.

Denno v. School Board of Volusia County (1997)

The law distinguishes between what's called pure speech and symbolic speech. Both are protected by the First Amendment. Pure speech is the spoken word, which is restricted if it constitutes what are known as "fighting words," or words meant to incite a riot. Symbolic speech, as seen in *Tinker*, is expressing yourself through objects, which may also be limited if determined to be disruptive.

• Should it be illegal to wear gang colors or symbols?

In an effort to control gang activity and crime, the City of Harvard, Illinois, made it illegal to wear gang colors or symbols, or to use hand signals. Thirteen-year-old Todd Gaut was out in public and wore a six-pointed star around his neck. When he saw the police, he tried to hide the star. They questioned him, and he admitted that he knew it was a gang symbol (for the "Action Packed Gangster

Disciples"). Todd was found guilty of breaking the law and was placed on **probation.** An Illinois appeals court found the law too broad and threw out Todd's conviction. Wearing certain clothing, even if some find it offensive, is protected symbolic speech, the court said.

City of Harvard v. Todd Gaut (1996)

• Is burning a U.S. flag a form of free expression and therefore legal?

The U.S. Supreme Court had another opportunity to address the issue of symbolic speech in 1989. Gregory Lee Johnson, a young adult, burned an American flag as a political protest during the 1984 Republican National Convention in Dallas, Texas. He was charged and convicted of desecrating (treating disrespectfully) the flag, a violation of Texas law. He was sentenced to one year in jail. The U.S. Supreme Court, in a five to four decision, reversed Gregory's conviction, stating: "If there is a bedrock principle underlying the First Amendment, it is that the government may not prohibit the expression of an idea simply because society finds the idea itself offensive or disagreeable."

Texas v. Johnson (1989)

• Can you be suspended for wearing a button with a slogan that school officials find disruptive?

During a teachers' strike, the high school in McMinnville, Oregon, hired replacement teachers. David Chandler's and Ethan Depweg's fathers were both teachers who joined the strike. High school students David and Ethan wore pro-strike buttons to school, including one that said: "We want our real teachers back." School officials found the buttons to be disruptive and asked the boys to remove them. When they refused, they were suspended for the rest of the day.

The buttons were determined not to be inherently disruptive. The Ninth Circuit Court of Appeals held that merely expressing a viewpoint by wearing a button wasn't an activity that would distract students or upset classroom order. The court said: "The classroom

prepares children for citizenship, and the proper exercise of the First Amendment is a hallmark of citizenship in our country."
Chandler v. McMinnville School District (1992)

GET ON THE CASE

● Are there places where or circumstances when your freedom of speech or right to express yourself is limited? What are they? Should there be limits at school? Why or why not?

● What do you think about participating in a peaceful demonstration? Is this something you've ever discussed with your friends or parents? What issue would you be willing to take a stand on? What type of demonstration do you think would be effective?

● Develop a campaign at school in support of an issue important to you—for example, against smoking or underage drinking. How might you act out your plan, gather support for your views, and bring them to the attention of the administration?

Can you dye your hair or wear a nose-ring to school?

Case: *Olff v. East Side Union High School District* (1972)

Suppose you want to get your nose pierced and dye your hair to match your school's colors. Does your school have any say about your personal appearance? Are school dress codes legal?

THE FACTS

In 1969, fifteen-year-old Robert Olff was a student at James Lock High School in San Jose, California. He did well in school and had a clean discipline record. At the beginning of the school year, the vice principal told Robert he couldn't go to class until he cut his hair. The school district had a regulation on personal appearance that stated: "Boys: Hair shall be trim and clean. A boy's hair shall not fall below the eyes in front and shall not cover the ears, and it shall not extend below the collar in back." The rule didn't restrict girls' hairstyles.

Robert and his parents challenged the rule in court, arguing that it prevented him from freely expressing himself—a guarantee of the First Amendment (see the **Bill of Rights** on pages 18–19).

YOU BE THE JUDGE

● Do you think schools have a right to restrict how students look or dress? Why or why not?

● Why do you think a school would be concerned with a student's appearance?

THE RULING

As Robert's case made its way through the courts, another lawsuit was filed in California. Lindahl King challenged the hair length regulations at a junior college. He and four other students tried to register at Saddleback Junior College, in Mission Viejo, California, and were denied because of their hair length. Because the issues and arguments were the same, the cases were considered together by the U.S. Supreme Court.

The school district, in Robert's case, argued that long hair on boys interfered with the educational process. Sworn statements from eleven teachers and administrators described the need for a hair regulation for boys. They said long hair tended to create a less serious atmosphere, more discipline problems and distractions, and "less education" in the classroom.

The first court ruled in Robert's favor. The federal trial court said the U.S. Constitution protects the freedom to determine your own hairstyle and personal appearance. The court ordered the school to allow Robert to attend without cutting his hair. He was a junior at the time he returned to school. But the school district disagreed with the court's decision and asked a higher court to consider the case. Two years later, the federal court of appeals reversed the trial court's decision. It decided school authorities have the right to develop a code of dress and conduct, without unconstitutionally infringing on the rights of students.

Robert and his lawyer took the final step and asked the U.S. Supreme Court to review the lower court's decision. The Court denied Robert's request; the decision of the lower court in favor of the school was left standing.

Because the U.S. Supreme Court decided not to get involved with managing schools, the rules regarding dress codes are left to the states and school districts. Private schools may establish their own rules, but public schools must balance individual student rights and the freedom of speech and expression with the school's responsibility to maintain a safe, peaceful campus. Dress code restrictions need to be reasonably related to an educational purpose.

When the U.S. Supreme Court decided not to consider Robert Olff's case, two of the justices disagreed and voted to hear it. Justice William O. Douglas wrote a brief opinion, stating in part: "Hairstyle is highly personal, an idiosyncrasy which I had assumed was left to family or individual control, and was no legitimate concern to the State. . . . One's hairstyle, like one's taste for food, or one's liking for certain kinds of music, art, reading, and recreation, is certainly fundamental in our constitutional scheme—a scheme designed to keep government off the backs of people."

He then concluded with: "The question tendered [by Robert's case] is of great personal concern to many, and of unusual constitutional importance which we should resolve." Justice Douglas, however, was in the minority. The Court hasn't yet considered the issue raised in Robert's case.

RELATED CASES

In addition to hair regulations, students have challenged other dress code restrictions. Students have wanted to wear Indian feathers or a kente cloth at graduation, or wear jewelry with religious symbols on it—and so the debate continues. The  cases discussed here give you an idea of the discretion courts have in deciding these issues. School authority takes priority over individual rights, if the school rule is reasonably connected to the goal of education.

• Can schools restrict how you express your religion?

In 1999, seventeen-year-old Crystal Seifferly sued Lincoln Park High School in Detroit, Michigan. She claimed the school's ban on wearing white power, gang, and satanic symbols violated her freedom to practice her Wiccan religion. Crystal wanted to wear a five-star pentagram as a religious symbol, but the school forbade it. The school also banned black nail polish, dog collars, and death-style makeup. Crystal and her lawyer reached an agreement with the school after a hearing in federal court. Before the court made its decision, the school agreed to change its policy and allow students to wear religious jewelry or other symbols of their spiritual beliefs.

• What about accessories that symbolize your heritage? Can these be restricted under a school's dress code?

In 1998, Aisha Price and Enockina Ocansey were told they couldn't wear a kente cloth during their high school graduation ceremony. The colorful sash symbolized their African heritage, but the dress code at the high school in Arvada, Colorado, prohibited any adornments to the traditional graduation cap and gown. The students were told they could wear the cloth before and after the ceremony.

Aisha, Enockina, and their parents asked the federal district court for an order allowing them to wear the cloth. The court ruled against Aisha and Enockina, and they agreed to follow the court's ruling.

The courts have upheld similar school dress codes. In 1996, three Oklahoma students were disciplined for the same issue. (They were ordered to serve thirty days in an alternative summer program, in order to receive their high school diplomas.) At their graduation, two of the students had worn the kente cloth and a third wore an eagle feather in honor of her American Indian heritage.

• Do school uniforms violate your freedom of expression?

A public school district in Texas passed a mandatory school uniform policy for all elementary, middle, and high school students. Its purpose was to promote school spirit, respect for authority, increase attendance, decrease disciplinary action, and lower drop-out rates. An opt-out provision was included for parents and students with religious or philosophical objections. A number of students objected to the overall policy and asked the court for relief. They claimed that uniforms coerced them to make a statement about compliance and respect for the school, thereby infringing on their right to free speech. Their parents objected to the interference in their right to raise and educate their children. The court sided with the school, calling the intrusion minimal and the goal of improving the educational process valid. Parents' rights in the public school setting may be subject to reasonable regulation.

Littlefield v. Forney Independent School District (2001)

Many educators in the United States see uniforms and dress regulations as a simple and inexpensive way to make schools safer. They maintain that baggy clothes make it easier for students to bring weapons or drugs into schools. Uniforms help curb these problems and allow school administrators to spot nonstudents on campus.

• Is it gender discrimination if a school places hairstyle restrictions on boys but not girls?

The length of eight-year-old Zachariah Toungate's hair was debated in a Texas case. Mina Elementary School in Bastrop, Texas, had a rule that limited the hair length on boys. Zachariah, a third-grader, was suspended until he cut his ponytail. After three days, he was allowed to return without cutting his hair but was placed in the in-school suspension program. This meant he was separated from other students, received individual lessons from a substitute teacher, and had no physical education, music classes, or extracurricular activities. After four months of this, and following a psychological recommendation, Zachariah began homeschooling with his mother.

Zachariah and his mother sued the school district, claiming gender **discrimination,** because the hair length rule didn't apply to girls. The court of appeals decided that Zachariah had been discriminated against and the rule had no legitimate basis. There was no evidence that Zachariah's hair had caused any disruption or affected school discipline in any way. The school was unable to show that the rule advanced any educational goal. Two years later, however, the Texas Supreme Court reversed the decision of the lower court, ruling that it was not discriminatory to have a different grooming code for boys and girls.

Bastrop Independent School District v. Zachariah Toungate (1996)

• Should courts even get involved with school dress and grooming code disputes?

Eighteen-year-old Austin Barber disagreed with his Texas high school's rule that restricted hair length and banned earrings on boys. Austin claimed that although he was a senior at the school, he was eighteen and therefore legally an adult. He argued that the school rules didn't apply to him.

The Texas Supreme Court disagreed, ruling against Austin. It reasoned that such matters should be dealt with by the parents, school boards, principals, and teachers. The court decided that a school grooming code doesn't require judicial intervention, saying: "We refuse to use the Texas Constitution to micro-manage Texas high schools."

Austin Barber v. Colorado Independent School District (1995)

• What about earrings? Can girls wear them even if they're banned on boys?

Ten-year-old Jimmy Hines, a fourth-grader at Caston Elementary School in Indiana, was asked to remove the earring he wore to school. When he refused, he was suspended. Rather than transfer to another school (an option given to him), Jimmy took the earring out and returned to school. He and his parents asked the Indiana court to set aside the school rule because it discriminated against boys (the policy didn't apply to girls). They also claimed that the rule denied Jimmy the right to express himself through his personal appearance.

Students aren't the only ones who may be required to follow a dress code. Employers may also restrict the appearance of employees, as long as the policy doesn't discriminate—for example, by placing more demands on women than men. Employers who have dress codes are usually trying to ensure that their employees present a professional image to the public. Today, however, more and more companies are loosening their dress code restrictions, allowing employees to dress in a more casual manner.

The Indiana Court of Appeals upheld the ban, indicating there was evidence supporting the school's dress code. The court found a rational relationship between the rule and the educational mission of the school. Citing safety, discipline, pride, attitude, attendance, and achievement as underlying reasons for the dress code, the school persuaded the court to let the policy stand.

Hines v. Caston School (1995)

• Can schools restrict the style of clothing students wear?

A New Mexico high school freshman, Richard Bivens, wore saggy pants to school which, he was told, violated the school dress code. On many occasions, he was told to follow the rule or face the consequences. Richard insisted that he "sagged" as an expression of his black culture. He was suspended for the rest of the semester for refusing to follow the rule. Richard and his mother asked the court to lift the suspension. The court refused, finding the dress code appropriate. It said: "Not every defiant act by a high school student is constitutionally protected speech."

Richard Bivens v. Albuquerque Public Schools (1995)

GET ON THE CASE

● Are you surprised this issue hasn't been decided by the U.S. Supreme Court? Why do you think that is? As the Texas Supreme Court said, is personal appearance any concern of the courts or should parents and schools resolve these matters?

● Do you think there should be rules regarding personal appearance at school? Is there a risk to student safety if no rules exist? Why or why not? What about gangs at school? Should bandannas, earrings, and other tokens of identification be restricted? If so, should the restrictions also apply to girls—even if it means not wearing certain colors of lipstick or nail polish? What are the pros and cons of mandatory school uniforms?

● Brainstorm with your classmates or friends about how kids in your school express themselves. For example, through their hairstyles or makeup, by wearing nose-rings or eyebrow rings, or by having tattoos. Which things on your list are sometimes disruptive in school? Why? Do you think these forms of expression should be banned in your school? Why or why not?

Can your student newspaper be censored?

Case: *Hazelwood School District v. Kuhlmeier* (1988)

You may keep a journal or write letters or email messages to family or friends, and there are no rules or restrictions on what you write—unless your parents have certain expectations of what's appropriate. At school, however, the situation is different. Your expressive activities, whether in writing, art, photography, or other mediums, can be reviewed by the school. They also may be limited if they don't meet the school's standards or if they're determined to be disruptive. This case sets the tone for school **censorship** of student expression.

THE FACTS

The school year was ending at Hazelwood School in Missouri. As the layout editor of the school paper, the *Spectrum,* Cathy Kuhlmeier put together the final issue with her staff. Leslie Smart was the movie critic, and Leanne Tippett a reporter and cartoonist. The newspaper was usually four to six pages and sold on campus for twenty-five cents.

One article in the final issue dealt with the impact of divorce on students. It named one student and quoted four others about their parents' behavior. A second article discussed teen pregnancy. It included the experiences of three unnamed students, but with enough details that students could identify them from the few pregnant teens at the school.

Before the paper was printed, the teacher who served as the newspaper's advisor asked the principal to approve the page proofs, a normal procedure. The principal pulled the two pages containing these articles. He found them to be inappropriate, highly personal, and too sensitive for the younger high school students. He was also concerned that, because it was the last issue of the school year, the people in the articles wouldn't have an opportunity to respond.

Cathy, Leslie, and Leanne, all seniors, disagreed with the principal's decision, claiming it violated their First Amendment right to freedom of expression (see the **Bill of Rights** on pages 18–19). They wanted to change the school policy that gave the principal authority to censor the paper. With their parents' help, the girls went to court to challenge the extent of editorial control a school may have over the content of a school newspaper.

YOU BE THE JUDGE

- Do you think the principal's decision violated the students' First Amendment rights? Why or why not?

- How much discretion do you think students should have over the content of the school newspaper or yearbook? Should the faculty or administration have any say about what's published?

- Do you think the students should have asked for consent from the parents of the students who were covered in the articles? Why or why not?

THE RULING

Before deciding whether the students' rights were violated, the U.S. Supreme Court discussed the nature of a school newspaper. The Court decided it wasn't a public forum—available for anyone to voice their opinion. Rather, it was a supervised learning experience for students interested in journalism.

The Court stated that education is primarily the responsibility of parents, teachers, and school officials—not the courts. A school isn't required to tolerate student speech that's inconsistent with its basic educational mission. Therefore, schools are allowed to control the newspaper's content within reason and to restrict other forms of student expression, including theatrical productions.

Justice Byron R. White wrote the majority opinion in *Hazelwood*, which is summed up best in these words: "[E]ducators do not offend the First Amendment by exercising editorial control over the style and content of student speech in school-sponsored expressive activities so long as their actions are reasonably related to . . . [a] . . . valid educational purpose."

> "[T]he First Amendment rights of students in the public schools are not automatically coextensive with the rights of adults in other settings, and must be applied in light of the special circumstances of the school environment."—*Hazelwood School District v. Kuhlmeier*, 1988

In a strong **dissent,** Justice William J. Brennan Jr. (with two other justices agreeing) argued that just as the public on the street corner must tolerate speech that tempts the listener to throw the speaker off the street, public educators must allow some student expression, even if it offends them or offers views or values that contradict those the school wishes to promote.

> "If all printers were determined not to print anything till they were sure it would offend nobody, there would be very little printed."—Benjamin Franklin (1730)

Leanne Tippett, now an environmental specialist with the State of Missouri, is married and has two daughters. Looking back on the case eleven years later, she said: *"Tinker* gave schools the authority to stave off anarchy, but *Hazelwood* went too far in limiting student expression. Someday another challenge may result in a more favorable decision to students."

Leslie Smart, who has worked as a journalist and in television, is now a teacher in Missouri. Although the student journalists lost their case, Leslie believes it was a worthwhile fight. She commented about the case, "Quiet, thoughtful, appropriate protest can be an effective way to get your voice heard."

The action taken by these students may not have changed censorship in schools, but it did open the subject for discussion. The Court's decision encourages schools to look closely at a student activity before imposing restrictions and to balance the school's goal of setting high standards for both student speech and the student's right to free expression.

RELATED CASES

The word *censorship* raises many eyebrows. The debate over censoring information continues in regard to books, music, newspapers, and the Internet. Something that may not be restricted in one place may be in the school setting. Your  school has the authority to reasonably limit or restrict the content of all forms of expression. This includes plays, the school yearbook, newspapers, and Web sites that may disrupt the school.

• How creative can you be in a creative writing assignment?

Douglas's eighth-grade English teacher at Oconto County Public School gave him a creative writing assignment to complete in class. Rather than beginning the assignment, Douglas visited with some friends and disrupted the class. He was sent out to the hall to finish his work. At the end of class he turned in a paper that described cutting off his teacher's head and putting it in a drawer. The teacher considered this a threat and reported it to the assistant principal. Douglas apologized, stating it wasn't meant to be a threat. He served an in-school suspension as a consequence.

The police filed charges against Douglas and he was found guilty of disorderly conduct and placed on one year of **probation.** Douglas **appealed** the decision to the Wisconsin Supreme Court, which ruled that written speech can constitute disorderly conduct depending on the content and circumstances. However, they agreed that Douglas's story did not constitute a true threat to his teacher, since it was written as part of a creative writing class and Douglas didn't have a history of violence. The conviction was reversed—his story was protected by the First Amendment.

In re Douglas D. (2001)

• Can a school censor something you did off campus?

Sixteen-year-old Brandon Beussink was a junior at Woodland High School in Marble Hill, Missouri. He created a Web page that criticized people in his school, including one of his teachers and the school principal. Although he created this Web page at home, school officials told him to remove it from the Web, which he did. A few students saw his site, but there was no evidence of any disruption at school. Yet, the school suspended Brandon for ten days. These missed school days were counted as absences, which brought Brandon over the limit for unexcused absences. As a result, he failed four classes that semester and faced the possibility of not graduating with his class the following spring.

Brandon filed a lawsuit, asking the court to restore his grades and to give him the chance to graduate with his class. He claimed the school had violated his free speech and he shouldn't be disciplined in school for comments he made off campus, even though they were in cyberspace.

The federal trial court agreed with Brandon and ordered the school to impose no further discipline against him. His ten-day suspension no longer could be counted as absences, which consequently reinstated Brandon's senior status. The court said that a function of free speech is to invite dispute—that free speech serves its highest purpose when it creates unrest or dissatisfaction with present conditions, or even stirs people to anger.

Beussink v. Woodland School District (1998)

• Can students restrict the type of advertisements that are accepted in student-run publications?

Natalie Berger and Dow-Chung Chi, high school seniors in Massachusetts, were co-editors of the Lexington High School yearbook. Ivan Chan, also a senior, was editor of the school newspaper, the *Musket*. Both publications were student-run and funded by sales and advertisements. They each had a policy of not running political or advocacy advertisements.

Douglas Yeo was a parent who lost a campaign against condom distribution at the school. He submitted ads to the school newspaper and yearbook advocating abstinence. Following their policy, Natalie, Dow-Chung, and Ivan decided not to accept the ads. They stuck to their position, even when the principal asked them to reconsider to avoid a lawsuit and media attention. After a number of meetings, the school left the decision to the students. The editorial judgment of the editors, acting independent of the school, was upheld by the Fifth Circuit Court of Appeals.

Yeo v. Town of Lexington (1997)

• Can material in an underground newspaper lead to school discipline?

Justin Boucher, a student at a high school in Greenfield, Wisconsin, wrote and distributed an underground newspaper called *The Last*. (He distributed the paper in school bathrooms, in school lockers, and in the cafeteria.) The June 1997 issue included an article titled "So You Want to Be a Hacker"—a how-to blueprint for invading the school's computer system. In the article, Justin not only encouraged doing this but also offered to "teach you more" after mastering the first lesson. Justin was suspended and later expelled for

endangering school property. Based on the reasonable forecast rule, which judges the likelihood of disruption based on recent events, substantial disruption of a school activity was possible and Justin's expulsion was upheld by the Seventh Circuit Court of Appeals.
Boucher v. School Board of Greenfield (1998)

• Can you be suspended for passing out an underground newspaper at school?

Cory Bystrom and Adam Collins attended a high school in Fridley, Minnesota. They distributed an underground newspaper called the *Tour de Farce*. Under school policy, school officials had the right to review any publication before it was distributed on campus; if the officials found it vulgar, indecent, or obscene, they could prohibit its school distribution. Cory and Adam were suspended for violating this policy. The students and their parents sued the principal and the school district for violating their right—to free speech at school. The court ruled in favor of the school, having determined the policy was reasonable.
Bystrom v. Fridley High School (1987)

GET ON THE CASE

- What is the purpose of a school newspaper? To incite and provoke, or to inform and entertain? Should there be any limits on student reporters and editors? Who decides where the line is drawn between acceptable and unacceptable journalism? What if your school or the school newspaper has its own Web site—should limits be set on its content? Should your school paper be sensitive to certain issues based on the age of the audience? Why or why not?

- What about a student's off-campus activities? Do you think the school ever has a right to restrict what a student does away from school? If so, under what circumstances?

● The *Hazelwood* decision has been criticized as giving too much authority to school officials and not adequately protecting a student's First Amendment rights. What do you think? Some states have passed laws further protecting high school journalists (including Arkansas, California, Colorado, Iowa, Kansas, Massachusetts, and Nebraska). You might want to check into the laws of your state to see if any exist regarding your rights as a journalist. Call your local newspaper and ask to speak with the reporter who covers education issues (major metropolitan papers have education sections and reporters who should be aware of the laws). Or go to the library or search the Internet to learn more about laws in your area.

● Interview the editor or advisor of your school newspaper. Has this person ever experienced censorship firsthand? If your school doesn't have a student newspaper, talk to the journalism or writing teacher about this issue.

ISSUE:

Can you be forced to say prayers at school?

Case: *Lee v. Weisman* (1992)

In 1636, Providence, Rhode Island, was founded as a place where families could freely practice their religion. Three hundred and fifty years later, a young girl from Providence, Deborah Weisman, and her parents continued the fight for religious freedom. Although the Constitution's principle of separation of church and state remains valid, it's been blurred in the school setting by recent cases and decisions. This case, and the decisions that followed, have shed further light on the religious freedoms you have as a student.

126

THE FACTS

It was June 1989, and fourteen-year-old Deborah Weisman was preparing to graduate from Nathan Bishop Middle School in Providence, Rhode Island. Her school district had a practice of inviting members of the clergy to the graduation ceremonies to offer a blessing and say a prayer. The district had written guidelines for composing a public nonsectarian prayer. A rabbi was invited to Deborah's graduation.

Four days before the event, Deborah and her father asked the school to cancel the rabbi's part of the ceremony. They argued that the public school, and therefore the state, was forcing students to participate in a religious exercise—a violation of the **Establishment Clause** of the First Amendment (see the **Bill of Rights** on pages 18–19). The school said it was too late to change the ceremony, and the event continued as planned. Deborah and her father then sued the school district to prevent future ceremonies from including prayers. She didn't want to face the same situation four years later at her high school graduation.

> "[T]he lessons of the First Amendment are as urgent in the modern world as in the eighteenth century when it was written."—*Lee v. Weisman*, 1992

YOU BE THE JUDGE

- Do you think including a blessing and a prayer in a graduation ceremony violates the separation of church and state included in the First Amendment? Why or why not?

- Do you think a school is promoting religion by including prayer in a ceremony? Why or why not?

THE RULING

The U.S. Supreme Court, in a five to four decision written by Justice Anthony M. Kennedy,
found that prayer at a graduation ceremony was a
state-approved religious exercise, in which the student was forced to participate. Although Deborah
could have chosen not to attend the ceremony and still receive her
diploma, the Court dismissed this option as unrealistic, saying:
"Everyone knows that in our society and in our culture, high school
graduation is one of life's most significant occasions."

In this case, the motives for prayer were good, but the danger
of promoting religion outweighed its benefits. The Court said
religious beliefs and expression are too precious to be prohibited or
ordered by the government—they are best left as private, individual
matters.

The Court summed up its interpretation of the Establishment
Clause by stating the development and preservation of religious
beliefs is an individual choice, with each person promised the freedom to pursue that choice. The Court also stated, in a few words,
the philosophy behind many First Amendment decisions: "[S]peech
is protected by ensuring its full expression."

The First Amendment begins with these words: "Congress shall make no law
respecting an establishment of religion." This phrase is referred to as the
Establishment Clause (this is where the concept of separation of church and state
comes from). It means that the government may not promote or affiliate itself
with any religious teaching or organization. Government may not advance or
inhibit religion, or aid, foster, or promote one religion over another. Federal and
state governments are to be neutral in all religious matters.

Religious freedom guaranteed by the First Amendment often collides with
the concept of separation of church and state. On one side is the position that
religious education and school prayer should exist in public school. Opponents
argue that school prayer of any sort conflicts with the Establishment Clause.

Deborah graduated from Hope High School in Providence, where no graduation prayers were said. When asked about her case in 1999, she noted: "Although not always easy, stand up for what you believe in. . . . What seemed like a small complaint about a commonsense issue became a situation which has had a great effect on me. I have truly come to understand, from reactions we received, that hatred often comes from ignorance."

In a similar case, where a "moment of silence" at school was prohibited, Justice O'Connor made this comment in her **dissent:** "It is difficult to discern a serious threat to religious liberty from a room of silent, thoughtful schoolchildren."

Taking a stand on something you feel strongly about may be difficult. Deborah and her family did so, and after several years, they succeeded in changing public school graduation ceremonies. The process may not always be smooth or risk-free, but positive change is worth the effort.

RELATED CASES

Although our country was founded on the belief of separating church and government activities, the debate continues to this day. And, as you'll see from the following cases, courts don't always agree with each other. A case may be decided one way in one **jurisdiction,** with the opposite result in another.

- **What if a prayer at a school function is voluntary and not required? Does it violate the separation of church and state in these instances?**

In Houston, a student named Pamela Jones, her father, and two other students and their parents challenged Clear Lake High School's policy of allowing seniors to voluntarily write and present an invocation at their graduation ceremony. (It was strictly a choice of the senior class and, if voted in, had to be performed by a volunteer from the class.) Past functions included references to Christianity, including the words *Lord, Gospel,* and *Amen.* After considering the U.S. Supreme Court ruling in *Weisman,* the federal court upheld the Texas policy—finding no violation of the Establishment Clause. The difference between this case and *Weisman* is that this one concerned a *voluntary,* not mandatory, activity arranged by students themselves.

Jones v. Clear Creek School District (1992)

• What about prayers at school sporting events?

In June 2000, the U.S. Supreme Court ruled against voluntary, student-led, student-initiated prayer at school football games. The Santa Fe School District in Galveston County, Texas, allowed students to read a prayer over the public address system at home football games. Several students and their parents objected to the policy, and the Court agreed that the practice violated the Establishment Clause. The Court ruled that the U.S. Constitution demands that schools not force students to choose between whether to attend the sporting events or to risk facing a personally offensive religious ritual.

Santa Fe Independent School District v. Jane Doe (2000)

• Can religious groups meet on school grounds?

Senior Emily Hsu and several of her friends asked their high school in Roslyn, New York, for permission to form an after-school Christian Bible Club and to meet on campus. The purpose of "Walking on Water" was to pray and study the Bible. The proposed rules of the club required all officers to be Christian. They were told this provision was unacceptable, and therefore the club couldn't form on campus. Emily and her parents sued the school district, the school superintendent, and district board members, claiming **discrimination**—denial of access to school facilities for her club.

Emily won in court based on the federal 1984 Equal Access Act. This law "guarantees public school students the right to form extracurricular groups that engage in religious, philosophical, or political discourse."

Hsu v. Roslyn Union Free School District (1996)

Note: In a 1990 U.S. Supreme Court case *(Westside Community Board of Education v. Mergens)*, the Court determined that a Bible club at school doesn't violate the Establishment Clause if other non-curricular groups are allowed and no school officials participate in the club.

And in 2001, the U.S. Supreme Court ruled that excluding a religious youth group from meeting at a public grade school after school hours amounted to unconstitutional **discrimination** based on the club's views. *(The Good News Club v. Milford Central Schools)*

• Can you hand out religious material on school property?

Tracy Hemry and Kristi Jones attended Wasson High School in Colorado Springs, Colorado. They identified themselves as Christian students and believed that part of their religious duty was to distribute their church publication, *Issues and Answers*, to their fellow students. The principal allowed the girls to distribute the publication on the sidewalk in front of the school but not on campus. The girls and their parents sued the school board, school principal, and superintendent, claiming a violation of civil rights by restricting distribution on campus.

The Colorado federal court decided the restrictions placed on the paper's distribution were appropriate, saying: "[T]he hallways of Wasson High School are not a public forum for indiscriminate use by the general public."

Hemry v. School Board of Colorado Springs (1991)

• Can advertisements for classes about religion be distributed at school?

Joseph Hills ran a nonprofit summer camp for elementary schoolchildren. The Scottsdale Unified School District had a literature distribution program that allowed outside groups to distribute promotional materials to its students. However, it excluded any material that was commercial, political, or religious. Mr. Hills's camp offered nineteen courses, including two called Bible Heroes and Bible Tales. After a complaint from a parent, the school district told Mr. Hills he could no longer distribute his brochures on campus. Mr. Hills took his case to court where he succeeded in proving what is called viewpoint discrimination. He argued that because the Bible classes were taught as history or literature, but not from a religious viewpoint, the school district violated his First Amendment rights by denying him equal access to the schools.

Hills v. Scottsdale Unified School District (2004)

• What if you want to give your classmates an invitation to attend a church meeting? Is this okay?

Andrew Muller was in fourth grade at Jefferson Lighthouse Elementary School in Racine, Wisconsin. He asked his teacher if he could hand out a flyer inviting the public to a religious meeting at his family's church. The principal told Andrew he couldn't hand out the invitation at school. The Seventh Circuit Court of Appeals agreed with the school's rules governing distribution of nonschool publications, saying: "School officials may impose reasonable restrictions on the speech of students, teachers, and other members of the school community."

Muller v. Jefferson Lighthouse School (1996)

• Can public schools have religious holidays as vacation days?

Chicago public school teacher Andrea Metzel didn't think Good Friday should be a school holiday, and she sued the state superintendent of education. Illinois state law allowed twelve holidays each school year—nine for nonreligious celebrations, two that are religious in origin (Thanksgiving and Christmas) but secularized, and Good Friday—a purely religious holiday, celebrated by believing Christians.

The Seventh Circuit Court of Appeals ruled that the law violated the Establishment Clause and was therefore unconstitutional. It said schoolchildren may be excused on religious holidays, but mandatory school closure in favor of one belief or religion is prohibited.

Metzel v. Leininger (1995)

On the other hand, the U.S. Supreme Court in January 2000 let stand a Maryland law that required public schools to close on Good Friday. The Court didn't comment on the case, leaving the issue unresolved among the states. The Court may take up the issue at another time, though, because a dozen states have similar laws. On the same subject, the Court (in March 2000) rejected a challenge to Indiana's designation of Good Friday as a state holiday.

• Is prayer at school acceptable if the majority of students are in favor of it?

At Wingfield High School in Mississippi, several students asked the principal, Dr. Bishop Knox, for permission to read a prayer each morning over the school's intercom. The school's student body voted 490 to 96 in favor of the prayers. After three days of allowing the prayer readings, Dr. Knox was suspended for the remainder of the school year by the school district's board of trustees. The court affirmed Dr. Knox's suspension due to his total disregard of the law—knowing that school prayer was unconstitutional.

Board of Trustees of Jackson School v. Knox (1997)

GET ON THE CASE

• Why do you think it's important, from the standpoint of the nation's courts, to keep religion out of public schools? Why was this dictate included in the First Amendment? Do you think the amendment should be reconsidered? Why or why not? What dangers might be posed by a repeal of this part of the amendment?

• Besides public schools, where else are religious events restricted? Why do you think this restriction is important for adults?

● Do you see any First Amendment violations in the situations listed below? How would you decide these issues? Discuss your answers and reasons in support of each. See the court decisions at the end of this section.

1. Kentucky state law required the Ten Commandments to be posted in every public grade school classroom.

2. Attendance was required at a human sexuality class by all students in public school in New Jersey.

3. A Maryland school board required students to say the Lord's Prayer or read from the Bible each morning.

4. Alabama allowed a one-minute moment of silence for meditation in public schools.

5. In West Virginia, students were to salute the flag and say the Pledge of Allegiance each morning at school. Noncompliance meant expulsion.

How the courts ruled in each case:

1. The main purpose of posting the Ten Commandments on schoolroom walls was plainly religious and therefore prohibited. *Stone v. Graham*, 449 U.S. 39 (1980)

2. "[T]he 'free exercise clause' was adopted to protect the one individual who is sincere in a conscientious religious conviction." Sex education classes are to be optional, not mandatory. *Valent v. New Jersey Board of Education*, 274 A.2d 832 (1971)

3. The daily prayer wasn't allowed, as the state must remain neutral in matters of religion. *Murray v. Curlett*, 374 U.S. 203 (1963)

4. The moment-of-silence rule was struck down—because it had a religious purpose. *Wallace v. Jaffree*, 472 U.S. 38 (1985)

5. A compulsory salute to the flag violates the principles and spirit of the First Amendment. *West Virginia Board of Education v. Barnette*, 319 U.S. 624 (1943)

ISSUE:

Do school officials have the right to discipline you?

Case: *Ingraham v. Wright* (1977)

While you're at school, your teachers and the school's administrators are responsible for making sure you learn a number of subjects. Because they also have this responsibility for the other students in your school, they may need to discipline you if you create classroom disruptions or break other school rules. Perhaps your school disciplines students by sending them to detention or by making them write an essay about their behavior. Or maybe you live in a state that allows **corporal punishment** in school. If so, you may have lots of questions about how this punishment is carried out and what your rights are under the law.

135

THE FACTS

James Ingraham was fourteen years old and in the eighth grade at Drew Junior High School in Miami, Florida. In October 1970, James was in the school auditorium, onstage with other students. A teacher thought James was being disruptive and told him to leave the stage. Because James was slow in doing so, he was taken to the principal's office to get five swats with a paddle. (This form of discipline was allowed in the school district.) James claimed he hadn't done anything wrong and refused to be paddled. Consequently, he was held down by two school officials while the principal gave him twenty swats. The paddle was about two feet long, three to four inches wide, and a half-inch thick. James suffered some bruising and required medical attention, which kept him out of school for ten days.

He and his mother sued the principal, assistant principal, and school superintendent, claiming the paddling violated James's Eighth Amendment protection against cruel and unusual punishment (see the **Bill of Rights** on pages 18–19). They also claimed James's **due process** rights were violated, because the school didn't hold a hearing or give James advance notice of the twenty swats he received.

YOU BE THE JUDGE

• Do you think paddling in schools is cruel and unusual punishment? (Remember, the school policy allowed it.)

• What about James's due process rights? Do you think he should have been given a chance to tell his side of the story before he was punished?

THE RULING

The U.S. Supreme Court considered both of James's claims in deciding this case. At the time, a national debate raged in the schools on whether corporal punishment could be used, or whether it violated the Eighth Amendment. The Court began by look-ing at the history of the Eighth Amendment and determined it didn't apply to discipline in public schools. In a five to four decision written by Justice Lewis F. Powell, the Court ruled that the Eighth Amendment was designed to protect convicted criminals only. The justices refused to extend its protection to situations outside crimi-nal cases.

> The *Ingraham* Court took a historical view of discipline at school: "The use of corporal punishment in this country as a means of disciplining school children dates back to the colonial period."

The Court, however, did state that teachers and principals must be cautious and use restraint when giving a physical punishment. The justices suggested using a test to determine if paddling is neces-sary, recommending the school should consider (1) the seriousness of the offense, (2) the student's attitude and past behavior, (3) the nature and severity of the punishment, (4) the age and physical condition of the student, and (5) the availability of a less severe but equally effective means of discipline. The school district should also create a school-wide policy on discipline and make sure everyone in the school is aware of it.

The Court also rejected James's due process argument. It decid-ed that because public schools are open to the community, students are sufficiently protected against abuse. Therefore, there's no need to hold a full hearing before disciplining a student.

On the other hand, the Court determined due process should be followed before suspending or expelling a student. Corporal pun-ishment is meant to quickly correct a student's behavior without interrupting his or her education. Suspension and expulsion have a greater impact on a student's education, requiring at least an informal "give-and-take between student and disciplinarian."

This case demonstrates that reasonable discipline at school doesn't violate the U.S. Constitution. The U.S. Supreme Court left this matter up to the states to address. State laws regarding discipline in school vary, so if you want to know more about your state's laws regarding this issue, check with your local police.

RELATED CASES

Not all states permit physical discipline at school. Where it is allowed, schools must consider whether the particular offense warrants such punishment or whether other methods of discipline would be more effective or fair. Schools must follow other procedures before using expulsion or suspension as discipline.

• Can you be suspended or expelled without a hearing?

Nineteen-year-old Dwight Lopez was a student at Central High School in Columbus, Ohio. The school had experienced some tension regarding Black History Month, such as racially motivated demonstrations, disorderly conduct, and property damage. Dwight was in the lunchroom when a few black students entered and started overturning tables. Dwight and his friends got up and left, taking no part in the activity. Dwight was suspended—but no reasons were given, and no hearing was scheduled. There was some confusion about the length of his suspension, and he stayed out a week longer than he was supposed to. After a month, the school transferred him to another school in the district.

Dwight, along with eight other students who'd been suspended from various schools in the district, took his complaint (that he was suspended without any notice or hearing) to court and ultimately won. The U.S. Supreme Court, in a five to four decision written by Justice Byron R. White, held that Dwight's due process rights were violated. In cases of suspension or expulsion, due process requires schools to give students notice and an opportunity to tell their side of the story.

Goss v. Lopez (1975)

• Can physical discipline in schools be considered assault?

Anita Holbrook was a fourth-grade teacher in Kentucky. When one of her students failed to complete an in-class assignment, she gave her three swats with a paddle. The girl was slightly bruised but by the next morning, her buttocks "didn't sting bad or hurt." Ms. Holbrook was arrested and convicted of assault. She **appealed** and her conviction was eventually reversed by the Kentucky Court of Appeals. It held that she wasn't reckless in her actions and that the student didn't suffer serious physical or mental harm. "A teacher is justified in the use of physical force within certain bounds," the court said.

Holbrook v. Commonwealth of Kentucky (1996)

Some states ban corporal punishment at school, including California, Hawaii, Illinois, Maine, Maryland, Montana, Nebraska, Washington, and Wisconsin.

• Can you be expelled for using a weapon in school?

D. B. was twelve years old when she got into a fight at school and stabbed another student. D. B. was expelled from all public schools in her county in Georgia. She and her parents asked the court to reverse this decision, arguing that it violated her right to a public education. The court ruled that the expulsion was valid due to the circumstances and zero tolerance for weapons at school. Although D. B. has a right to a free public education, she doesn't have an absolute right to attend a public school. She may be required to attend an alternative program or be homeschooled.

D. B. v. Clarke County Board of Education (1996)

• What about having a fight? Can you be expelled for this?

At a Friday night football game at Eisenhower High School in Decatur, Illinois, six members of two rival gangs were involved in a violent fight in the stands. Although there were no guns or knives used, innocent bystanders were injured by fists and feet and were forced to flee the area to avoid serious injury. Each student involved was expelled for two years for violating school rules. The school board later reduced the penalty to the remainder of the school year with an opportunity to attend an alternative program. The students sued, arguing that the zero tolerance policy was racially motivated, they were stereotyped as gang members and racially profiled by the school board, and expulsion was excessive since no weapons or drugs were involved. They requested immediate reinstatement. The court ruled that as long as the students were given a chance to be heard—due process was followed—the school's zero tolerance for violence was valid. The expulsion was upheld by the court.

Fuller v. Decatur Public School Board (2000)

• If you're expelled or suspended, does the school have to provide an alternative education program?

R. M. and B. C. of Washakie County, Wyoming, were caught selling marijuana to other students on school grounds. Their school expelled them for the remainder of the year, and they were ruled **delinquent** by the juvenile court and placed on **probation.** As part of the probation orders and at the students' request, the judge ordered the school district to provide them with an alternate educational program during their expulsion period. The district objected to this order and appealed. The appeals court ruled that the school district has a compelling interest in providing a safe and secure environment. All juveniles must be given an opportunity for an education, but they are not entitled to disrupt or endanger the educational process. A student can temporarily forfeit his schooling through his own conduct. R. M. and B. C.'s request for alternative education was denied.

R. M. and B. C. v. Washakie County School District (2004)

GET ON THE CASE

- Should teachers and the administration be granted immunity from lawsuits or prosecution for disciplining students? Who determines when the line has been crossed and a student's rights have been violated?

- Is in-school suspension an effective disciplinary tool in your school? Is it taken seriously by teachers and students? If not, what would you suggest in those cases that don't merit suspension or expulsion?

- Interview a local attorney—either a prosecutor or a defense attorney—about the issue of discipline in school. What has this person's experience been with this issue? Does he or she think the laws need to be changed? Can this person offer any stories from personal experience? If you find it difficult to arrange such a meeting, ask a teacher to invite an attorney to visit your class and talk about the law and discipline.

- Assemble a panel of people who are knowledgeable about discipline in the school. You could invite your school principal, school board members, teachers, students, parents, and police officers. Work with your class to develop a specific list of questions to be addressed. Hold the panel discussion during class or in the evening, as an informational event.

Can your parents discipline you however they see fit?

Case: *Joshua DeShaney v. Winnebago County Social Services* (1989)

If you act out at home or school, do your parents discipline you? That's what parents often do to help their children learn the difference between right and wrong, and between what's acceptable and unacceptable. The law respects parents' right to discipline their children; however, there *are* limits. Courts, by looking at what's reasonable under all the circumstances, decide whether parents have crossed the line. Although this case is about a young child, the ruling applies to all **minors,** including teens.

THE FACTS

Four-year-old Joshua DeShaney lived with his father and his father's girlfriend. Over a two-year period, nurses, police officers, and the department of social services made and received numerous reports about Joshua being physically abused at home. At one point, Joshua was removed from his father's home but was returned three days later. (His father agreed to see a counselor and enroll Joshua in pre-school, but he didn't follow through.) Then, in March 1984, Joshua was hospitalized with severe brain damage. He was in a coma, and bruises covered his body. Although he survived, he's permanently paralyzed and mentally disabled now.

Joshua's mother, Melody DeShaney, sued the Winnebago County Department of Social Services in Wisconsin for returning Joshua to his father. She argued that the department had a duty to protect her son from his father and should now be held responsible for the abuse.

YOU BE THE JUDGE

- Do you think the county should be held respon-sible for what happened to Joshua? Why or why not?

- Is the government responsible for protecting children from their parents?

THE RULING

In a six to three decision written by Justice William H. Rehnquist, the Court held that the government doesn't have a "constitutional" duty to protect chil-dren from their parents. Therefore, the department wasn't at fault and couldn't be held responsible. Joshua's father caused the boy's injuries, and he was prosecuted and sent to prison as a result.

The U.S. Constitution doesn't require states to protect the life, liberty, and property of its citizens from acts by private individuals. The government is prohibited from doing certain things without affording you **due process,** but the government isn't required to guarantee you protection from others.

> Although the government isn't *required* to protect children, all states assume this responsibility under **child protection laws.** Social services departments exist to provide services for families, and the departments have a duty and a responsibility to protect children when they're in their care—but not while the children are in a *parent's* care. However, even when children are removed from a parent's home, the government has only a limited liability if something goes wrong.

The U.S. Supreme Court has consistently respected parents' rights to discipline their children. Recognizing that each state's civil and criminal laws must be followed (there are no federal laws regarding parental discipline—it's a matter left to the states to legislate), the Court has deferred to state and local **jurisdictions** to do just that—enforce their laws regarding the protection of children. Unfortunately, these protections aren't always enough to prevent harm to children by their parents.

RELATED CASES

Excessive discipline in the home may amount to child abuse, which is illegal in all states. But determining what's excessive and what's acceptable isn't always easy. Because individual parents hold a wide range of beliefs on how to best raise  their children, children are disciplined in many different ways. And some parents might never even consider using some forms of discipline that are legal, such as spanking.

• Can parents use unlimited physical discipline because of their religion?

Eleven-year-old Adam lived with his father in Franklin County, Iowa. After a number of reports of physical abuse, Adam was removed from the home by Child Protective Services. His father **appealed** this decision and claimed that he practiced **corporal punishment** as part of his religion. The court didn't accept this argument. It said that while laws allow parents to use moderate and reasonable physical discipline with their children, they may not cross the line and physically abuse their child, for religious or other reasons.

In re A. O. (2002)

• What if your parents spank you so hard that you're bruised afterward? Is this against the law?

R. A. lived with her father and stepmother in Iowa. When she was nine years old, her father spanked her with a leather belt, which left bruises on her buttocks and thighs. The bruises were still visible three days later when she reported the abuse to her family therapist. Her father was convicted of **child endangerment** and sentenced to 180 days in jail. He **appealed** and the Iowa Supreme Court stated that a parent's right to discipline his or her child "clearly has its limits." When they're exceeded, the parent may be criminally liable. However, the court noted: "American courts are not in full agreement on how to define the limits of the parental right to discipline a disobedient child."

State v. Arnold (1996)

• Can your parents discipline you using a paddle or switch?

Eight-year-old Amanda lived with her mother and visited her father, a noncustodial parent (meaning he didn't have custody). One weekend, her father told her to wash her hair, bathe, and get ready for some photographs. Because Amanda wasn't ready when her father arrived, he spanked her three times with a wooden spoon over her denim jeans. Red marks were visible for several days.

Amanda's father was charged with and convicted of child abuse. He appealed, arguing that his actions did not constitute child abuse,

and the Iowa Supreme Court ruled in his favor. The court decided that parents "have a right to inflict reasonable corporal punishment in rearing their children." It also said that "welts, bruises, or similar markings are not physical injuries *per se*."
Hildreth v. Iowa D. H. S. (1996)

> In most states, child abuse, endangerment, and assault are considered a **felony** with jail or prison time possible.

> "Parental autonomy is not . . . absolute. The state is the guardian of society's basic values. . . . the state has a right, indeed, a duty, to protect children. State officials may interfere in family matters to safeguard the child's health, educational development, and emotional well-being."—*In re Phillip B.*, 1979

GET ON THE CASE

- What forms of discipline do your parents use? Do you think these rules or punishments are effective? Why or why not? What would you suggest as alternatives?

- With your mom or dad, develop a fair discipline plan for your home. List the rules of your household and the consequences for breaking them. Post the rules where everyone in the family can see them.

- How do you balance a parent's right to raise a family with a child's right to protection from abuse? Do you think parents have too little or too much freedom concerning discipline? Teachers, medical professionals, social workers, and other people who are responsible for children have a legal responsibility to report suspected abuse or neglect. What do you think about these laws? Should they be extended or limited in any way? Why or why not?

ISSUE:

Can you be hospitalized for mental health treatment against your will?

Case: *Parham v. J. R.* (1979)

Do parents know best when it comes to raising their kids? Are their decisions always right? Regardless of mistakes parents may make in child-rearing, the law gives them a certain amount of authority over their kids. But along with this authority comes a high level of responsibility concerning your health and well-being. This case explores the rights children have to challenge their parents' decisions and get their opinions heard.

THE FACTS

When J. L. was six years old, he was expelled from school for two months. He received outpatient therapy and was eventually diagnosed as having a "hyperkinetic reaction to childhood." His mother and stepfather then asked a mental health hospital to admit him indefinitely. The physician who interviewed J. L. and his parents before he was admitted to the hospital said J. L. was uncontrollable and aggressive. J. L. was admitted to the hospital and after several unsuccessful attempts to return him home (his parents said they couldn't control him), his parents signed papers surrendering custody of the boy to the county. J. L. remained in the hospital for several more years, even though the hospital recommended at one point that he be moved to a special foster home. A lack of funds prevented the move. When he was twelve, J. L. and another boy, J. R., took legal action to change their situation.

At only three months old, J. R. had been placed in foster care because of his parents' neglect. He spent the next seven years in seven different foster homes. In 1970, he was diagnosed as borderline retarded, mentally ill, unsocialized, and aggressive, and he was placed in a mental health hospital. Three years later, the hospital recommended that J. R. be moved to a foster home or an adoptive home because "he will only regress if he does not get a suitable home placement, and as soon as possible." Two years later, J. R. was thirteen and still under hospitalization.

J. L. and J. R., along with their attorneys, filed a lawsuit representing approximately 140 children and teenagers in mental health institutions in the state of Georgia. They sued James Parham, the director of the state's mental health programs, and the medical director of the hospital where the boys were confined. The basis of their suit was that the procedures in Georgia allowing a parent or **guardian** to hospitalize a **minor** without his or her consent violated the minor's **due process** rights.

YOU BE THE JUDGE

● Should parents have the right to commit their child to a mental health hospital against his or her wishes? Why or why not?

● Who should have the final say on whether a child remains hospitalized—a parent or the hospital? Why?

● How does a child's due process right fit into this decision? Should the child have the right to express his or her opinion? If so, how much weight should this opinion have in the decision to place the minor in a psychiatric hospital?

THE RULING

In making its decision, the U.S. Supreme Court first looked at Georgia's state law on committing children to psychiatric hospitals and whether the procedures protected children from unnecessary hospitalization. The law allowed parents to apply for hospitalization, which was reviewed by the hospital superintendent. This person could admit any child for "observation and diagnosis"—usually for a few days. If, during this stay, an evaluation showed that the child had a mental illness and was in need of treatment, the child would be hospitalized until a doctor determined that the child was no longer a threat to self or others.

> States have different laws about the length of hospitalization. Some set a maximum length of stay depending on the final diagnosis. For example, if the person is a danger to himself or herself, the stay is three months; if the person is a danger to others, the stay is six months, with regular reviews scheduled.

The Court then studied the admission procedures at each of Georgia's mental health hospitals, as well as the child's right to not be hospitalized and to receive treatment in a less restrictive setting.

Although the Court recognized that parents are responsible for raising their own family, it found that they alone don't have the authority to institutionalize their child. Before hospitalization, an independent medical evaluation must show the need for inpatient treatment. In a six to three decision written by Justice Warren E. Burger, the Court concluded that without the opinion of a neutral person, minors may be unnecessarily hospitalized.

In a **concurring opinion,** Justice Potter Stewart pointed out that not only does commitment to a mental institution result in loss of liberty, but the person is also affected by the stigma attached to treatment in a mental hospital. Consequently, hospitalization must be accomplished through procedures that comply with due process. An independent evaluation, with regular reviews of the patient's condition and the patient's right to be heard at an impartial hearing, must be in place.

When a child in psychiatric care turns eighteen, he or she may remain hospitalized but must proceed through the adult commitment process—the patient isn't automatically discharged due to age. An adult can be hospitalized against his or her wishes through the **civil commitment laws,** which vary by state.

In upholding Georgia's process for voluntary commitment of children by the parent, the Court declared that an independent process that includes a thorough psychiatric investigation, followed by periodic reviews of the child's condition, would protect children who shouldn't be admitted. The boys lost the case.

On the balance between parent and child in the decision-making process, the Court wrote: "Simply because the decision of a parent is not agreeable to a child or because it involves risks does not automatically transfer the power to make that decision from the parents to some agency or officer of the state. . . . Most children, even in adolescence, simply are not able to make sound judgments concerning many decisions, including their need for medical care or treatment."

If you, a family member, or a friend is hospitalized for mental health care, you may have questions about the rights of patients. For example: What happens to your privacy or your ability to communicate with the outside world? Do you retain any rights while in treatment, or is it like being in jail?

The laws in each state differ slightly regarding your specific rights while in treatment. In general, patients have privacy rights and the use of personal possessions and storage space. You may be allowed to wear your own clothes and will have the opportunity to make telephone calls (to a limited number of approved people), write letters, and have personal visits during certain hours. Depending on the circumstances, these rights may be suspended or restricted to protect your safety or the welfare of others. You may also have the right to refuse certain types of treatment, such as shock therapy, psychotherapy, or extreme behavior modification programs. There are also laws that protect you from unreasonable restraints (mechanical, isolation, medication). A violation of your rights may result in civil or criminal penalties. A local lawyer or librarian can point you to the law in your **jurisdiction.** If you're going into treatment, ask the doctor or hospital staff for a written copy of your rights as a patient.

Teenagers and children no longer have to worry about being locked up in a mental hospital and forgotten. States now have procedures and policies for admission, interviews, evaluation, and periodic reviews for continued care. Patients' rights apply to minors, as well as their parents and other adults. Outpatient counseling is another alternative available to teens. Your parents may arrange for counseling, and as long as you're a minor under your parents' authority, you have to go. In some states, you may find your own counselor and attend counseling without your parents' knowledge or consent. Laws extending these rights are usually limited to drug counseling and health care regarding sexually transmitted diseases and contraceptives.

RELATED CASES

Because one person isn't solely responsible for committing someone into a mental health facility, it's highly unlikely that a child would be wrongly hospitalized. Although parents have a certain

degree of authority to make mental health decisions for their children, a nonrelated, neutral decision-maker who has evaluated the minor determines whether confinement for mental health treatment is necessary. After treatment, and at a point at which the person is no longer a danger to self or others, he or she may receive a less restrictive placement (like a foster home).

- **Are your parents violating your civil rights if they force you into a psychiatric hospital, or do they have a duty to make sure you receive such care?**

At her mother's request, seventeen-year-old R. J. D. voluntarily entered a hospital in Birmingham, Alabama, for drug screening and counseling. After four days, she was released. Her mother then placed R. J. D., against her will, in the secure ward of a psychiatric hospital. Two weeks later, her father smuggled her out. (Her parents were divorced.) She and her father sued the hospital and the admitting psychiatrist, claiming false imprisonment and violation of R. J. D.'s civil rights. The Alabama Supreme Court held that a parent may seek medical care for a child against the child's will. The court also noted that parents have a legal responsibility to care for their child; failing to do so may result in civil and criminal penalties. R. J. D.'s claims were dismissed.

R. J. D. v. Vaughan Clinic (1990)

- **If you break the law, does your mental state matter?**

Lionel was charged with the murder of his playmate, six-year-old Tiffany, in Pembroke Park, Florida. He was twelve years old when he inflicted multiple, fatal injuries to Tiffany's head and upper body. Lionel explained it was an accident and he was imitating professional wrestling moves he had seen on TV. It was known that Lionel had a mental age of a nine- or ten-year-old and that he had no previous experience with the judicial system. His case was **transferred** to adult court, and Lionel was found guilty of first-degree murder and sentenced to life in prison without the possibility of parole.

Lionel **appealed** and the higher court reversed his conviction and sentence. The Florida court ruled that the trial court was wrong in not determining before Lionel's trial whether he was mentally competent. In other words, did Lionel understand the charges filed against him and could he help his lawyers with his case? Lionel later plead guilty to second-degree murder.

Tate v. State (2003)

Individual states have different laws about rights to mental health treatment and care. For example, some states give minors the right to seek treatment without their parents' consent or the right to refuse treatment. In Wisconsin, minors who are fourteen and older may receive treatment if their parents refuse to arrange for mental health services. In Iowa, if the parent seeks help for the child and the child refuses, the matter goes to juvenile court for a decision.

GET ON THE CASE

- Have your parents ever forced you into doing something you didn't want to do? How did that make you feel? Did you understand their reasons? If so, did that help you accept their demand? If some time has passed since this incident, do you feel differently now than you did at first?

- Do you think minors should have a voice in all decisions concerning their health? Why or why not? What if a child has a life-threatening disease, such as AIDS or cancer? What roles should the child and his or her parents have in deciding on medical care? Does it matter how old the minor is? Why or why not? What if an alternative therapy is being considered? Who should have the final say in which treatment to use?

ISSUE:

Can your grandparents visit you against your parents' wishes?

Case: *Parkerson v. Brooks* (1995)

Times change, and with change comes new laws. Grandparents' visitation rights weren't as big of an issue ten years ago, but they are today. Because of the nation's high divorce rate and the larger number of blended families in the country, courts are facing many more custody and visitation questions.

Balancing the rights of family members and other loved ones with the best interests of the children involved isn't always easy or clear-cut. The right solution in one case may not make sense in another, as you'll see in the cases that follow.

THE FACTS

Under Georgia's grandparent visitation law, Mrs. Parkerson asked the court for an order allowing her to visit her four-year-old granddaughter (her daughter's child). The child's parents, Stacy and William Brooks, wanted the court to deny the visitation request. The Brooks had decided that it wasn't in their daughter's best interests to see her grandmother and that the law invaded their right, as parents, to raise their child without government interference.

YOU BE THE JUDGE

- Do you think the Georgia law was unconstitutional? Do grandparents have a right to see their grandchildren even if the parents object?

- Should parents have the final say regarding who their children see and don't see? Or, put another way, should grandparents or other relatives be able to force contact with family members?

- Do you think the government has a right to interfere with the way parents raise their children?

THE RULING

The Georgia Supreme Court determined that the law was unconstitutional, because it violated the parents' right to raise their children without state interference under the Fourteenth Amendment (see page 165). An **appeal** by Mrs. Parkerson to the U.S. Supreme Court was unsuccessful. The Court declined to review the Georgia court's decision. This left the Georgia Supreme Court decision in effect.

In deciding whether Mrs. Parkerson could obtain court-ordered visitation with her granddaughter against the wishes of the girl's parents, the Georgia Supreme Court reviewed the history of parent and child relationships under the law. The court studied cases dating back to 1923 and found a common thread—state interference with parents' rights to custody and control of their children is permissible only when the health or welfare of a child is threatened. Otherwise, the law protects the authority of the immediate family.

As a result, the court found that parents in Georgia, as well as parents throughout the United States, have a fundamental right to raise their children as they see fit, without excessive government intrusion. The court was also worried that forcing children to spend time with someone against their parents' wishes would negatively affect the children.

Quoting from an earlier Georgia case, the *Parkerson* court also stated: "[T]he law's concept of the family rests on a presumption that parents possess what a child lacks in maturity, experience, and capacity for judgment required for making life's difficult decisions."

So, although the court understood that grandparents can enhance a child's life, it stood by tradition in its decision, saying: "Having found wisdom, learned patience, and journeyed in faith, many grandparents have much to give their grandchildren in the way of a vision of the world, as models of action, and may, as well, provide children with a very profound sense of connection with others. However, as important as grandparents can be in the lives of their grandchildren, the relationship between parent and child is paramount."

When contacted in 1999, Stacy Brooks noted that cases such as theirs can be hard on families: "When an agreement cannot be reached regarding visitation of grandparents, and the judicial system becomes involved, everyone needs to first weigh the financial cost, and emotional toll of a courtroom battle on an already strained relationship."

The issue of visitation, as you'll see in the related cases, has been expanded beyond just your parents. Whether you have a say in who you visit depends on your state's law. Every state has a grandparent visitation law, with different rules and requirements. Your chance to go to court and talk with the judge is better as you get older. Once you reach your teens, the court will want to know your wishes on such matters. The judge may speak with your lawyer, if you have one, or talk to you directly. If you get to appear in court, take advantage of this opportunity to tell the judge how you feel and why.

RELATED CASES

During the past twenty-five years, courts have split over the issue of grandparent visitation. Some have ruled on the side of parents' rights, while others have held that grandparent visits may occur—even over parents' objections. As you'll see in the following cases, visitation rights are also being sought by siblings, stepparents, aunts and uncles, and people who aren't related to the child in question.

> In 2000, the U.S. Supreme Court considered the constitutionality of Washington State's grandparent visitation law. The Court's decision upheld the fundamental right of parents to make decisions concerning the care, custody, and control of their children. The Washington case involved the children of Brad Troxel, a man who committed suicide in 1993. Brad wasn't married, but he left behind two young daughters, Natalie and Isabelle. Brad's parents, Gary and Jenifer Troxel, obtained a court order under the Washington grandparent law, granting them one weekend each month with the girls. Their mother, Tommie Granville, later married and her husband, Kelly Wynn, adopted the girls in 1996. Tommie opposed the court-ordered visitation, arguing that it violated her authority over the girls' lives. The Supreme Court of the State of Washington agreed and ruled that the law was an unconstitutional invasion of parents' rights. The U.S. Supreme Court agreed. *Troxel v. Granville* (2000)

• Do you have an automatic right to visit your underage siblings?

Louise was six years older than her half-brother Pierce. They were both in foster care in different homes in Franklin County, Massachusetts. Louise had a long history of psychological problems and hospitalizations. Her monthly visits with her brother were stopped when it became apparent that Pierce was psychologically harmed by them. Pierce was adopted and the plan for Louise was long-term foster care. Through her attorney, Louise asked for post-adoption visits with Pierce. The Massachusetts Court of Appeals denied her request but did state that the issue could be renewed at a later date as the children got older and Louise's behavior improved.

Although state law provided for sibling visitation, it is not an absolute right. The best interests of both siblings must be weighed before implementing a visitation schedule.
In re Adoption of Pierce (2003)

> On the other hand, a South Dakota court wrote "it is universally recognized that in the absence of compelling reasons to the contrary, the best interests of siblings require that they be raised together whenever possible." The court said this also applies to half-siblings. Although this statement was issued in a custody case, the principles apply to visitation issues as well. "Family unity between siblings often promotes their best interests," the court said. *Crouse v. Crouse* (1996)

• Do people who are gay or lesbian have any legal rights to their partners' children?

In 1999, the U.S. Supreme Court was presented a case involving visitation between a birth mother, L. M. M., and her former same-sex partner, E. N. O, a couple in Massachusetts. The women had been together for thirteen years and had agreed to jointly raise a child. Through artificial insemination, L. M. M. became pregnant and gave birth to Baby O. M. in February 1995. In 1998, the couple's relationship began to deteriorate, and they separated that spring. L. M. M. would no longer allow E. N. O. to see the child, who was now three years old. E. N. O. went to court, seeking enforcement of their agreement to jointly raise O. M. Based on their three-year history as a family, and the psychological best interests of O. M., the Supreme Court of Massachusetts gave E. N. O. visitation with O. M. The court noted that the only family O. M. had ever known had broken up and the child was entitled to be protected from further trauma of the separation of his parents. The U.S. Supreme Court didn't accept the case for review, meaning the decision of the Massachusetts court stands.
E. N. O. v. L. M. M. (1999)

• What about relatives who help raise a child? Do they have any visitation rights?

Michelle Guchereau asked her sister and brother-in-law, Cindy and Richard LaHaye, to care for her one-year-old daughter, Josie, while she served a jail sentence. This involved Michelle giving the couple temporary legal custody of Josie. Cindy and Richard, who lived in Louisiana, ended up keeping Josie for fourteen months.

When Michelle was released from jail, she moved to Chicago and sought sole custody of Josie. Based on Josie's best interests, the Louisiana court granted Michelle's request, but against her wishes granted liberal visitation to Josie's aunt and uncle—up to six days on each alternating holiday (Christmas, New Year's, Easter, and Thanksgiving), three weeks each summer, and weekly telephone access with the child.

In the Interest of Baron (1996)

• What legal rights do stepparents have to see their stepchildren?

Eight-year-old Cody lived with his father and stepmother in Coconino County, Arizona. His mother had visitation on alternating weekends and one night each week. Cody's stepmother had been part of Cody's life for over two years when his father died in a traffic accident. Cody went to live with his mother who stopped contact with his stepmother. The stepmother asked the court for permission to visit Cody. The appeals court ruled that the test to be applied is whether the child viewed his stepmother as a parent and whether the stepmother and child had formed a meaningful relationship over a period of time.

Riepe v. Riepe (2004)

• Can grandparents be denied visitation with their grandchildren if the courts don't approve of their behavior?

Missouri resident Leah Mack had three children, Christina (age five), Arthur (age one), and William (one month). Leah's mother, Bernice E. Young, had a court order to visit the children on alternating weekends, on holidays, and during two one-week periods each summer. Due to increasing problems between the grandmother and Leah's husband, Leah asked the Missouri court to reduce the visitation order. Among other things she disapproved of, the grand-mother brought her mother to the visits, and this woman spoke neg-atively about the children's father. According to the visitation order, the grandmother was prohibited from smoking around the children, which she did anyway. Christina returned from visits smelling of tobacco smoke; she pretended to smoke with a stick or pencil; and on one occasion, she reported that she'd been burned with a cigarette. The grandmother also took Christina to a halfway house to visit a relative, against Leah's wishes. All in all, the court deter-mined the grandmother's conduct harmed the parents' authority and restrictions were appropriate. Visits with Christina were limited to once a month for six hours; visits with the boys were restricted to once a month for one and a half hours at their parents' home.

D. F. S. v. Ellis (1994)

• Do adoptive parents have to continue contact with a child's birth family?

In 2005, the Wyoming Supreme Court denied the paternal grand-parents' request to visit their granddaughter who had been adopted by her maternal grandparents. Under the law, the adoptive parents may cut off all ties with the biological family.

Hede v. Gilstrap (2005)

• Do death-row inmates have a right to see their children?

W. G. T., a prisoner on Florida's death row, wanted to see his son, who lived with his aunt and uncle. The Florida District Court of Appeals held that supervised visits were possible but only if the boy's therapist approved. W. G. T. was entitled, however, to pho-tographs and regular reports about his son's health, education, and overall well-being.

W. G. T. v. B. C. (1996)

- **What if a parent uses illegal drugs? Does this affect his or her visitation rights?**

During a paternity trial in Washington State, Michael Waters argued that the court's restrictions placed on his visits with his son, Alex, were unreasonable. Michael admitted to using alcohol and cocaine in the past. The Washington court also found that he had committed acts of domestic violence and that his daily use of marijuana could negatively affect Alex's general welfare. The court withheld visitation until Michael provided thirty days of drug-free urine samples. The court didn't accept his argument that his religion encouraged his daily drug use.

State v. Waters (1998)

GET ON THE CASE

- What other circumstances might lead to visitation disputes? How do you think the court would rule on such cases, based on what you've read here?

- Are your parents divorced? If so, are you satisfied with your visitation arrangements? What type of challenges are involved? Are there any changes you'd like to make?

ISSUE:

Do you have any rights if you break the law?

Case: *In re Gault* (1967)

Even if you break the law, you still have rights. The court system has been carefully set up to protect those accused of a crime and to be sure that people in power—such as police officers, lawyers, and judges—don't abuse their authority. The court system recognizes the importance of treating people humanely and with a certain level of respect while they're involved with the courts. This means being fair, allowing people to tell their story, and helping them make their way through a system they may not understand.

THE FACTS

On June 8, 1964, fifteen-year-old Arizona resident Gerald Gault made an indecent telephone call to his neighbor, Mrs. Cook. She reported the call to the police, who traced it to Gerald's house. Gerald, who was already on **probation** for theft, was picked up by the police and arrested. Gerald's parents were at work and weren't told of their son's arrest or of any charges filed against him. Two **delinquency** hearings were held during the week before a juvenile judge, which Gerald attended without the assistance of an attorney. He didn't have an opportunity to question Mrs. Cook because she failed to attend the hearings. Gerald and his parents weren't given a copy of the charge against him (obscene phone calls) or told what may happen to him. On June 15, the judge determined, based on the testimony of Gerald's **probation officer,** that Gerald was a **delinquent** and ordered that he attend the state reform school (today called the Department of Juvenile Corrections) until he turned twenty-one. This was for an offense that, if committed by an adult, carried a two-month sentence.

Gerald and his parents **appealed,** claiming the laws and procedures for **minors** who got into trouble were inadequate. Gerald wasn't provided his Fourteenth Amendment right of **due process**—specifically, he wasn't able to confront his accuser in court; he wasn't given any legal assistance; and his parents weren't notified of the charges.

YOU BE THE JUDGE

- Do you think Gerald's case was handled fairly? Should the courts and police have made sure Gerald's parents knew about his arrest and the case against him? Why or why not?

- Was the sentence Gerald received reasonable, especially considering the sentence an adult would have received for the same crime? Why or why not?

- Should Gerald have been given the chance to confront Mrs. Cook about her version of the incident?

THE RULING

In deciding Gerald's case, the U.S. Supreme Court reviewed the sixty-year history of juvenile law in the United States. In a seven to two decision written by Justice Abe Fortas, the Court concluded that juvenile court procedures must be fair and follow due process guidelines. In other words, Gerald and his parents shouldn't have been kept in the dark about the charge against Gerald, and Gerald should have been given an opportunity to tell his side of the story in court, with the help of a lawyer. The Court noted that the possibility of losing one's freedom is as significant (if not more so) to a minor as to an adult. The Court looked at each step in Gerald's original case and made three separate rulings:

1. **Notice of charges**—Defendants must be told of the charges far enough in advance to allow them a reasonable amount of time to prepare for the court proceeding. This means the court should have ensured Gerald's parents knew about the case.

2. **Right to counsel**—Minors who are suspected of breaking a law should receive an attorney's help in court.

3. **Confrontation, self-incrimination, cross-examination**—The right to face your accusers and question them (**cross-examination**), as well as your right to remain silent, is guaranteed by the Fifth Amendment (see the **Bill of Rights** on pages 18–19). The Court couldn't find a reason why juveniles shouldn't have these rights. Gerald should have been afforded all of these rights before being sent to the state school for boys.

In the first *Gault* decision by the Arizona Supreme Court (before the case went up to the U.S. Supreme Court), Justice Charles C. Bernstein commented on the purpose of juvenile courts: "Juvenile courts do not exist to punish children for their transgressions against society. The juvenile court stands in the position of a protecting parent rather than a prosecutor. It is an effort to substitute protection and guidance for punishment. . . . The aim of the court is to provide individualized justice for children . . . [and] authoritative treatment for those who are no

Continued ⟶

longer responding to the normal restraints the child should receive at the hands of his parents. The delinquent is the child of, rather than the enemy of society, and their interests coincide."

Finding that due process had not been followed in Gerald's case, the U.S. Supreme Court reversed the Arizona Supreme Court decision and sent the case back with an order to follow due process. Gerald spent five months at the reform school and was released.

The U.S. Supreme Court's position regarding the rights of juveniles was clear from several comments by Justice Fortas. He wrote: "Neither the Fourteenth Amendment nor the Bill of Rights is for adults alone." The Fourteenth Amendment to the U.S. Constitution uses several phrases that apply to every U.S. citizen, regardless of age: due process and **equal protection.** Again, due process, in its simplest form, means fairness. Gerald wasn't treated fairly—his opportunity to defend himself or even know what he was charged with was limited. Equal protection is the principle that everyone in the same group or classification should be treated the same. A person can't be singled out of a group and treated differently.

Gerald Gault was a Job Corps student in California when the decision in his case was announced. He later became a computer technician, joined the army, and served in Korea. He's married and has two sons. When interviewed twenty-five years later, he commented: "I had no rights, but now my children and the children of the community have rights—the right to an attorney and to be able to question their accuser. It was well worth the fight."

Fourteenth Amendment, Section 1.: All persons born or naturalized in the United States, and subject to the **jurisdiction** thereof, are citizens of the United States and of the State wherein they reside. No State shall make or enforce any law which shall abridge the privileges or immunities of citizens of the United States; nor shall any State deprive any person of life, liberty, or property, without due process of law; nor deny to any person within its jurisdiction the equal protection of the laws.

In the 1800s, children were tried, convicted, and sentenced as if they were adults. Children who were abandoned or neglected were institutionalized. The concepts of rehabilitation, treatment, and best interests brought about the first juvenile court in Chicago, Illinois, in 1899. At this time, the emphasis shifted to providing services for children and teens rather than simply locking them up. Sixty-eight years later, the U.S. Supreme Court in *Gault* fully recognized minors as people with specific rights when charged with a crime. Juveniles in the justice system were now afforded the same rights as adults. The *Gault* decision still applies to all minors facing criminal charges.

RELATED CASES

The test used most often by the courts in determining whether a person's statements to police are admissible evidence (can be used at trial) is "totality of circumstances." In other words, all factors surrounding the statement or confession are considered. These include age, maturity, ability to communicate, criminal history, mental and physical state, and environment at the time of questioning. The following cases offer examples of admissible and inadmissible statements.

- **If you confess to a crime but your parents aren't with you, can the confession be used against you in court?**

Sixteen-year-old Andre was involved in a fistfight at Pueblo High School in Tucson, Arizona, and was sent to the principal's office. His mother and the police were called to the school. The police also wanted to talk to Andre about a sawed-off shotgun found in another student's car. When his mother arrived, the police were already questioning Andre. They refused to allow his mother to enter the room.

Andre admitted to possessing the gun on school grounds. He later plead guilty to possession of a deadly weapon on school grounds and possession of a firearm as a minor. He was placed on probation for one year. He appealed, and the Supreme Court of Arizona ruled that Andre's confession should not have been used against him because his mother was not allowed to be present during questioning. She was not disruptive or threatening and the charges did not involve her. She should have been present to ensure her son understood his rights. Andre's conviction was reversed and the judgment of guilt vacated.

In re Andre M. (2004)

• Does your age and background affect whether your confession is admitted as evidence?

Michael Alvarado was seventeen years old when he and Paul Soto tried to steal a truck at a shopping mall in Santa Fe Springs, California. Paul approached the driver and when he refused to cooperate, Paul shot and killed him. Michael was on the passenger side of the truck at the time. About a month after the shooting, Michael was asked to come to the police station for an interview. His parents brought him and waited in the lobby while Michael and an officer went to an interview room. Michael was not advised of his rights before or during the two-hour interview. He was asked twice if he wanted to take a break. He was not under arrest and no threats or promises were made. Michael confessed to the killing by Paul and his part of the attempted car theft. He and Paul were convicted of second-degree murder and attempted robbery. Michael was sentenced to fifteen years to life in prison. On appeal he challenged the admission of his confession, arguing that he was in custody and not given his **Miranda** warnings.

Miranda requires a two-part analysis of a police interrogation: what were the circumstances surrounding the questioning and would a reasonable person have felt free to stop the interview and leave. The U.S. Supreme Court has not mandated that a juvenile's age or inexperience with law enforcement be considered. The U.S. Supreme Court ruled that Michael was not in custody when his statements were made and therefore they were admissible at his trial.

Yarborough v. Alvarado (2004)

• Does Miranda apply to everyone who questions you?

Ira, age thirteen, and three friends were charged with assaulting a classmate with a rock. The beating took place after Ira got off the school bus at the end of the day. The assistant principal of Duggan

Middle School in Springfield, Massachusetts, interviewed each of the boys and Ira admitted hitting the victim. However, Ira argued that his admission should not be used against him because he was not advised of his rights by the assistant principal. The Supreme Judicial Court of Massachusetts rejected Ira's position, stating, "School officials acting within the scope of their employment . . . are not required to give Miranda warnings prior to questioning a student in conjunction with a school investigation." Ira was not in police custody and the assistant principal was not acting for the police.

Commonwealth v. Ira I. (2003)

• What if you confess, but the police didn't follow the rules?

Fifteen-year-old Jacqueline Montanez was arrested in Illinois on May 13, 1992, for the murders of Hector Reyes and Jimmy Cruz, committed the day before. The victims had been shot in the head. Jacqueline was taken to the police station at 9 p.m. and read her Miranda rights. Police called her mother at 10 p.m. and told her that Jacqueline was involved in a murder and was in protective custody. She asked to see her daughter and was told that they'd let her know when she could. At 2 a.m., her mother went to the station and waited until 8 a.m. to see her daughter. In the meantime, police had questioned Jacqueline throughout the night without the presence of an attorney, and at 6:15 a.m. she signed a written confession. A jury in Chicago, Illinois, found Jacqueline guilty, and she was sentenced to life in prison.

Jacqueline appealed, arguing that her confession was involuntarily obtained since she was questioned throughout the night, without a parent being present, and without being told she would be tried as an adult. The Illinois Court of Appeals found that the police had violated Jacqueline's rights in their attempt to obtain a confession. She should have been allowed to have her mother with her during questioning and should have been given the opportunity to ask for the assistance of a lawyer. Her conviction was reversed, and a new trial was ordered without her confession as admissible evidence.

People v. Montanez (1995)

• Can the police do whatever they want to get you to confess?

In an Illinois case, ten-year-old V. L. T. was found guilty of involuntary manslaughter in the death of a twenty-two-month-old child she was baby-sitting. She was sentenced to five years of probation. V. L. T. was taken into custody around 10 p.m. while in her pajamas. She had little food, drink, or sleep. She asked for her grandmother, who got to see her around 3 a.m., after V. L. T. had given a written confession. The Illinois Court of Appeals ruled that her confession was involuntary, considering all of the circumstances (she was deprived of sleep, proper clothing, and contact with her grandmother, even though she asked to see her). The confession therefore couldn't be used as evidence.

In re V. L. T. (1997)

GET ON THE CASE

- Where do parents fit in when a teenager becomes involved with the court? Do parents need to be involved with their child's **probation officer** and help in rehabilitation, or should the parents leave this matter entirely to the court system?

- Why should a child's parent be with him or her during police questioning? Do you think the presence of a parent might affect the questions asked? The way they're asked? Or perhaps the answer the child gives?

- Role-play an interview between police officers and suspects at the police station. (Some of the role-players can be the police, while others act as suspects, parents, or attorneys.) If possible, interview an actual police officer or legal expert to learn more about how such questioning is conducted.

ISSUE:

Does the whole world have to know about a mistake you made as a teenager?

Case: *Josh Davis v. Alaska* (1974)

Let's face it, everybody makes mistakes. That's how we learn. Yet some errors in judgment carry greater consequences than others—just ask anyone who's ever seen the inside of a police station. If you get in trouble with the law before you're eighteen, your case is usually handled by a juvenile court and kept confidential. However, this doesn't necessarily mean that your record will be sealed forever or destroyed when you turn eighteen.

170

THE FACTS

Richard Green's mother asked him to run an errand. On his way to the store, the sixteen-year-old saw two men standing by a blue car, along a little-used side road. Richard asked them if they needed any help; when they said no, he continued on to the store. On his way back, he saw them again. This time, one of the men was standing near the trunk of the car, holding a crowbar.

Later that day, Richard and his stepfather discovered a safe on the road where the blue car had been parked. They called the police and were both interviewed. Richard explained what he saw and later identified the two men in police photos. It turns out someone had broken into a local bar and stolen a 200-pound safe containing more than $1,000 in cash and checks. When Richard and his stepfather found the safe, its bottom had been pried open and it was empty. Police eventually found the blue car at Josh Davis's home. Paint chips and insulation from the safe were found in the trunk.

Richard's testimony and identification of Josh Davis was important to the state's case. However, Richard was a **minor** on **probation** for an unrelated burglary. Josh's lawyer wanted to question Richard about his criminal background in court and argue that Richard quickly and falsely identified Josh, so the police wouldn't consider him a suspect. He knew his probation would probably be revoked if he was thought to be involved with the crime.

> If a person breaks the terms of his or her probation, the court may impose more serious consequences, such as time in **detention** or stricter probation conditions.

The Alaska trial court didn't allow Josh or his attorney to bring up Richard's history or the fact that he was on probation at the time of the burglary. Josh was found guilty. He **appealed,** asking the U.S. Supreme Court to set aside the conviction since his right to **confrontation** was limited.

YOU BE THE JUDGE

- Do you think Richard's right to privacy (of his juvenile record) outweighed Josh's right to **cross-examine** him in court? Why or why not?

- Why did the Alaska court refuse to allow Richard's history to be presented at the trial?

THE RULING

Although this case is named after Josh Davis, he wasn't the person the U.S. Supreme Court was concerned with. Josh was tried and convicted of burglary and theft. During the trial, Josh's lawyer wanted to tell the jury about Richard Green's criminal record and probation, so they'd have a reason to question his credibility as a witness—a reason to suspect that he was lying.

The U.S. Supreme Court discussed the purpose of confrontation at trial, looking at the Sixth Amendment, which gives criminal defendants a right to confront witnesses in court (see the **Bill of Rights** on pages 18–19).

The goal of cross-examination is to challenge the accuracy of a witness's memory and to reveal any bias or prejudice he or she has toward the defendant or ulterior motives for a given testimony. Because Richard's testimony was critical to the case against Josh, the Court ruled that Josh's lawyers should have been allowed to ask Richard questions that might show a bias. The jury should have been given the opportunity to judge Richard's trustworthiness after knowing all the facts, not just some of them. In a seven to two decision written by Justice Warren E. Burger, the U.S. Supreme Court ruled that limiting the examination of Richard was an error. The case was sent back for a new trial.

The U.S. Supreme Court did make a point of saying that the right to confrontation isn't unlimited. They held that there's a duty to protect the juvenile from questions designed merely to harass, annoy, or humiliate.

Josh Davis was later convicted of possession and sale of heroin, and sentenced to twenty years in prison.

RELATED CASES

There's some truth to the expression that the past may come back to haunt you; the mistakes you make while growing up may ripple through your adult life. Fewer than 10 percent of America's teenagers are involved with the justice system. Most will become law-abiding, responsible adults. Even so, some will carry with them the scars of their earlier years—the effects of having a juvenile record.

• Does your school need to know about your past trouble with the law?

N. P., a Louisiana resident, had been in gifted classes since the first grade. When he was fourteen, the school bus driver caught him with a gun. N. P.'s friend had stolen the gun from N. P.'s older brother, who was a security guard. His friend gave the gun to N. P. and asked him to return it to his brother. N. P. was expelled from school and charged with carrying the gun. He was placed on probation for two years. One of his probation terms required that he tell the principal of his new school about his probation and provide the name and phone number of his **probation officer.** N. P. objected on grounds of confidentiality.

Because this probation requirement was intended to ensure N. P.'s continued progress in school, the juvenile court didn't consider the disclosure to the principal to be a violation of confidentiality. The court said it served a legitimate purpose and wasn't intended to harass or jeopardize N. P.'s future.

State in the Interest of N. P. (1989)

• Can your juvenile record affect later adult sentences?

As an adult, Steven LaMunyon was convicted of marijuana possession with intent to sell and sentenced to three to ten years in prison. When determining Steven's sentence, the Kansas court considered

his juvenile offenses—two thefts, a burglary, and property damage—which increased his adult sentence. Steven argued it was unconstitutional to punish him as an adult for crimes he committed and had been punished for as a juvenile. The Kansas Supreme Court disagreed and upheld the sentence, stating that Steven was considered a repeat offender and his sentence was based on his criminal history, not on the specific offenses he committed as a minor.
State v. LaMunyon (1996)

• Can DNA blood tests required for an offense as a minor be held on file after you're eighteen?

In 1996, two juveniles in Arizona were charged with and plead guilty to child molestation. At sentencing, each boy was put on probation and placed at a residential treatment center. They were also ordered to submit to DNA blood testing, the results of which would be filed with a local law enforcement agency. Both teens and their lawyers challenged this part of their sentence. They claimed an invasion of privacy and sought protection from use of the test results after they turned eighteen. The Arizona Court of Appeals ruled against them on both counts. It stated that the primary purpose of DNA testing is to guard the public safety and that this outweighs the minor inconvenience in obtaining the blood sample. Furthermore, it said that ordering DNA testing isn't a form of punishment, and the records of such may be kept beyond a minor's eighteenth birthday. (Similar rulings have been made in the case of mandatory HIV and AIDS testing, following sex offense convictions.)
Appeal in Maricopa County Juvenile No. JV-512600 (1997)

• Does the media have a right to attend juvenile hearings?

J. E. W. was sixteen when he was arrested for murder and theft in Arizona. The prosecutor wanted to try him as an adult, and a hearing to decide this issue was scheduled. The news media asked for and received the court's permission to attend the hearing. J. E. W. appealed, asking that the hearing be closed to the media and general public. J. E. W. lost his appeal. The Arizona Supreme Court determined that the public has an interest in knowing how a juvenile court works and that they operate fairly and effectively. Closed or private hearings create suspicion about the court's operation.
Wideman v. Garbarino (1989)

• Can your juvenile records be released to the media?

Lee Boyd Malvo was seventeen in 2002 when he was charged with multiple crimes in several states stemming from a three-week series of sniper attacks in the Washington, D.C., area. Ten people were allegedly shot and killed by Lee and his co-defendant, forty-one-year-old John Allen Muhammed.

As the case against Lee progressed, a number of media organizations asked the Maryland court to unseal Lee's previous juvenile records and court transcripts of the proceedings. Public interest in this frightening and high-profile case was great. However, Lee's case in Maryland was kept in the juvenile court, which is required to balance public interest against the interest of the juvenile in being protected from stigma and preserving the potential for rehabilitation. The federal district court of Maryland permitted some of the requested documents to be released while keeping more specific information sealed. (Lee was being tried as an adult in Virginia and much of the information sought by the media in Maryland had already been disclosed in Virginia.)

In Virginia in 2004, Lee was tried and convicted by a jury on one charge of murder and unlawful use of a weapon, and he later plead guilty to another count of murder and one count of attempted murder. The Virginia court sentenced him to life in prison without the possibility of parole. (Since Lee was a minor at the time of the murders, he was not eligible for the death penalty.)

In re Washington Post (2003)

GET ON THE CASE

- What do you think of the decisions in these cases about juvenile records? Should the mistakes of your teen years be buried in the "graveyard of the forgotten past," as one court put it? Or should you have to live forever with the consequences of breaking the law? Should the type of crime committed play a role in this decision? Why do you think a juvenile's criminal record is treated differently than an adult's record?

• What about using a person's juvenile record to increase the sentence of an adult? Is this fair? Why should a shoplifting conviction at age fourteen affect a sentence at age twenty? On the other hand, if your only offense was the shoplifting when you were fourteen, shouldn't your record be cleared now that you're twenty, responsible, and independent?

• In most states, juveniles and adults who are found guilty of a sex offense are subject to a number of health and safety requirements. They may be ordered to register with law enforcement as a sex offender. At the victim's request, they may also be ordered to submit to an HIV test or provide a DNA sample for law enforcement information purposes. What do you think of the long-term effect of sex-offender registration and DNA testing? Should there be a limit on how long an offender is subject to these state laws? Or does the overall best interests and protection of the community justify permanent application? Talk this over with your friends and teachers. You could also ask the community relations department of your local police station to talk to your class about such laws in your community.

Can you request a jury of your peers?

Case: *McKeiver v. Pennsylvania* (1971)

A jury is a group of six to twelve people who have been brought together to decide a particular case. The jury listens to the evidence and arguments of the two sides, considers the law that applies to the case (which the judge tells the jury about), and reaches a verdict. Jurors are usually comprised of ordinary people, but they have an awesome responsibility.

THE FACTS

Three teenagers were in Fairmont Park in Philadelphia, Pennsylvania, when they were approached by a group of twenty to thirty boys. One of the boys, who was on a bike (sixteen-year-old Joseph McKeiver), demanded money from the teens. When one of the victims refused, Joseph punched him. The victim then gave Joseph a quarter, and he rode off. The victim later identified Joseph as the thief in this incident.

Joseph, who had never been arrested before, was charged with robbery, larceny (theft), and possession of stolen property. He plead not guilty, and the case was set for trial in the juvenile court. Joseph requested a jury trial, which the court denied. His case was tried by a juvenile court judge who found him guilty and placed him on **probation.** Joseph **appealed** this decision, arguing that his Sixth Amendment rights (see the **Bill of Rights** on pages 18–19) were violated because he was denied a trial by jury.

YOU BE THE JUDGE

- Do you think Joseph had a right to a jury trial? Why or why not?

- Do juvenile courts have to follow the same rules as courts for adults?

"Teen court" or "peer court" is a high school program where students become the judge, prosecutor, defense attorney, and jury. A teenager who's a first-time offender may appear before the teen court. This program is usually limited to nonviolent, **misdemeanor,** or low **felony** crimes. The offender must admit responsibility for the offense, and the teen jury decides the consequences. If the consequence is completed successfully and on time, no formal charges are filed in juvenile court. Consequences may include writing a paper on a particular subject, completing community service work, paying **restitution,** or writing a letter of apology to the victim. The offender may also be required to serve

Continued →

once or twice on a teen court jury. Participants in teen court are trained by local attorneys, **probation officers,** and judges. The use of teen or youth courts is growing in the United States, with more than one thousand such courts in existence by 2005. To learn more, see the National Youth Court Center at *www.youthcourt.net.*

THE RULING

Before addressing the main issue in this case, the U.S. Supreme Court reviewed earlier Supreme Court decisions about juvenile rights: the use of a juvenile's confession as evidence, **waiving** a **minor** into adult court, and the level of proof required to convict a minor. The Court concluded that minors aren't guaranteed all of the rights adults receive in the adult criminal process, including the right to a jury.

Over the years, courts and legal scholars have expressed different views on the use of juries in juvenile court. In previous cases, some of the justices thought jury trials were a fundamental right of the criminal justice system in the English-speaking world. Justification for juvenile court juries also was argued in cases where the minor was charged with a crime that, if the person were an adult, would be triable by jury.

Depending on the type of case, a defendant may prefer a jury over a trial before a judge alone. The theory is that it may be easier to convince a few jurors of your position than a single trial judge. The decision to ask for a jury, or not, should be made after consulting with a lawyer.

The Court in *McKeiver* needed to strike a balance between the different responsibilities of the juvenile courts. On the one hand, juvenile courts need to make minors realize they're in a serious situation. A jury could help provide a dose of reality to minors. On the other hand, juvenile courts need to be informal, as the philosophy of juvenile justice is treatment and rehabilitation, not punishment. The Court determined that of all the **due process** rights that could be applied in juvenile court, the right to a jury was the one that would most likely disrupt the unique nature of the juvenile process. In fact, the Court said: "[T]he addition of the trial by jury might well destroy the traditional character of juvenile proceedings."

However, Joseph's attorney argued that juvenile proceedings are very similar to criminal trials held in adult court and, therefore, minors should have the same rights as adults. The Court stuck to its position that juvenile proceedings aren't criminal prosecutions and that juvenile due process requires fundamental fairness. It wrote: "[O]ne cannot say that in our legal system the jury is a necessary component of accurate fact-finding." A trial before a judge alone is sufficient.

Several justices **dissented** in this decision (the vote was four to three), voting to grant juveniles the right to a jury. Equating the court experience of adults with juveniles, Justice William O. Douglas wrote: "The experience of a trial with or without a jury is meant to be impressive and meaningful. The fact that a juvenile realizes that his case will be decided by twelve objective citizens would allow the court to retain its meaningfulness without causing any more trauma than a trial before a judge. . . . Who can say that a boy who is arrested and handcuffed, placed in a lineup, transported in vehicles designed to convey dangerous criminals, placed in the same kind of cell as an adult, deprived of his freedom by lodging him in an institution where he is subject to be transferred to the state's prison and in the 'hole' has not undergone a traumatic experience?"

Although the U.S. Supreme Court didn't give minors an automatic right to a jury trial, it didn't go so far as to prohibit states from allowing juries in juvenile court. It stated: "If, in its wisdom, any State feels the jury trial is desirable in all cases, or in certain kinds, there appears to be no impediment to its installing a system embracing that feature. That, however, is the State's privilege and not its obligation."

If you're called to jury duty someday, you'll hear several terms, including *voir dire, challenge,* and *sequester.*

In order to select an impartial (unbiased) panel to hear and decide the case, the lawyers and judge involved will ask you questions about yourself. This is voir dire, which is a French term meaning "to speak the truth." Voir dire takes place during the jury selection process—at the beginning of the case. You'll be asked to state your name, age, occupation, family status, whether you've been on a jury before, and whether you know anyone involved with the case. More specific questions relating to the case will then be asked. The purpose of voir dire is to determine whether you have any bias or prejudice that may affect your decision-making ability.

After voir dire, the lawyers are given a chance to strike or challenge a set number of jurors. For example, if a group of twenty people went through voir dire, and a jury of twelve is needed for the case, each lawyer will be allowed to strike four people from the group. This would leave a panel of twelve to be sworn in to hear the case. Reasons for striking a panel member aren't required to be given.

In certain cases, jurors are kept together night and day during the trial—known as sequestering the jury. The court bailiff is responsible for your living arrangements—where you eat, sleep, and relax when you're not in court. Once the case is over and you've reached a verdict, the judge thanks you for your service and sends you home. Sequestering a jury is rare; it's only done in high-profile cases that have extensive media coverage. The costs and the level of inconvenience often dictate whether a jury will be sequestered.

RELATED CASES

People who are tried before a jury learn to appreciate the role of a jury. But there are other ways of experiencing the jury system. Juries are used in both criminal and civil cases. You may be called as a victim or a witness to testify before a jury. Your  chances are even better of being summoned to jury duty. It's both a duty and an honor to participate in government by sitting on a jury. The cases presented here discuss the function of a jury and your right to one in particular situations.

• If a state allows minors to have jury trials, do the jurors also need to be under eighteen?

In a Minnesota case, sixteen-year-old J. K. B. was charged with ter-rorist threats, assault, unlawful possession of a handgun, and pos-session of stolen property. His case was moved to adult court, and he was given the option of having a jury trial.

Although J. K. B. and his lawyer agreed that juveniles don't have a constitutional right to a jury trial, they claimed that since Minnesota extended this right to minors when they were tried in adult court, the jury must be made up of the defendant's peers—meaning other sixteen- and seventeen-year-olds. The Minnesota Court of Appeals didn't accept J. K. B.'s argument, saying: "A juror must have the maturity and understanding to do what may often be an unpleasant task." J. K. B. was found guilty by the jury (made up of legal adults) on all counts.

Welfare of J. K. B. (1996)

• Are juvenile proceedings and criminal prosecutions the same thing?

In an Oregon case, thirteen-year-old Brad Reynolds was charged with sexual abuse and giving obscene materials to a minor. He asked the court for a jury trial, which was denied. Brad was found guilty and sentenced to two years of probation. He and his lawyer appealed, claiming that the trial phase of the juvenile proceeding was, in fact, a criminal proceeding, entitling Brad to a jury.

The Oregon Supreme Court reviewed the history of juries in Oregon, noting the differences in how **juvenile delinquents** were treated in the 1800s versus the 1900s. More than one hundred years ago, children were treated the same as adults and could therefore have a jury trial. Since then, the philosophy of juvenile court has changed from punishment to rehabilitation. Juvenile justice often focuses on reforming and protecting.

The court also discussed the ideas behind juvenile hearings as opposed to adult criminal proceedings, saying: "The message of the juvenile code is clear . . . rehabilitation of children in trouble is a family affair." This isn't the case in adult criminal court, where punishment and deterrence are the goals. Consequently, the court determined that a juvenile trial isn't a criminal prosecution. The ruling of the lower court was upheld.

State v. Reynolds (1993)

• Does the possible sentence for breaking a particular law determine whether an adult has the right to a jury trial?

In a California case, Jerry Nachtigal, a legal adult, was charged with driving under the influence of alcohol in a national park. Jerry asked for a jury trial and was refused. He appealed, claiming that this decision violated his Sixth Amendment rights (see the **Bill of Rights** on pages 18–19). The U.S. Supreme Court disagreed. In 1993, the Court decided that the right to a jury trial doesn't always exist but depends on the seriousness of the offense. If the crime is serious enough that the law demands a maximum sentence of longer than six months, then you may request a jury trial or you may decide to waive this right. If the possible sentence is for less than six months or is considered a **petty offense,** your request will be denied. Because the maximum penalty for Jerry's crime was six months in jail, he was denied a jury trial. (He was fined $750 and placed on one year of probation.)

This ruling applies only to legal adults—people who are eighteen or older, unless you live in a state that allows jury trials for minors. States that currently provide for juries in some juvenile proceedings include Alaska, Arizona, Colorado, Kansas, Massachusetts, Michigan, Montana, New Mexico, Oklahoma, Texas, West Virginia, Wisconsin, and Wyoming.

U.S. v. Nachtigal (1993)

GET ON THE CASE

- Do you think teens who are sixteen and seventeen years old should be allowed to serve on juries? In your opinion, do teenagers have the experience and wisdom to sit in judgment of another person—teen or adult? Or should teens be limited to participating in teen court? Is age eighteen much different than seventeen or sixteen? Or should the age be raised to twenty or twenty-one?

● Are you ready to serve on a jury? Why or why not? How do you think your life experiences would help you in deciding the fate of someone else? If you're eighteen, maybe you've already been summoned for jury duty. If so, what did you think of the experience? Did you find it difficult to decide the case or vote because someone close to your age was on trial?

● Play the role of a journalist and write an article about a teen or peer court. Interview local participants, including the jurors, the teens on trial, and the judges. If you can't find a peer or teen court in your area, visit a neighboring city. You may need special permission to attend the court session.

ISSUE:

Can a teenager be sentenced to death?

Case: *Roper v. Simmons* (2005)

Murder is a **capital crime.** This means it's a crime that may be punishable by death. Whether you personally support the death penalty, it's a reality in thirty-eight states in our country. What does this mean for teens who commit horrific crimes and are **transferred** to adult court? At what age is a person fully accountable for a capital crime and therefore old enough to be sentenced to death?

THE FACTS

In 1993, seventeen-year-old Christopher Simmons developed a plan to rob and kill someone. He talked two friends, Charles Benjamin (fifteen) and John Tessmer (sixteen), into joining him. He convinced them they could get away with the crime because they were **minors.** The three teens met late one night, but John went home before the other two set out for the victim's home. Christopher and Charles broke in to Shirley Crook's home, tied her up, and took her to a nearby park in Fenton, Missouri. After putting a towel over her head and wrapping it in duct tape, they threw her off a bridge. She drowned in the water below.

Christopher bragged to a friend about what he did and was arrested at school the next day. He confessed to the murder and was tried as an adult and convicted. (The case against fifteen-year-old Charles was kept in juvenile court.) Although Christopher had no previous criminal record, the jury recommended the death penalty and the trial judge agreed. Christopher **appealed,** claiming protection by the Eighth Amendment's prohibition against cruel and unusual punishment (see the **Bill of Rights** on pages 18–19). His attorney argued that since minors are not considered responsible enough to use alcohol, serve on juries, or even see certain movies, then they should not be held to a higher level for their crimes and they shouldn't be subject to the death penalty. The state also used Christopher's age in its argument *for* the death penalty, stating: "Isn't it scary" that a seventeen-year-old is capable of such horrific acts?

YOU BE THE JUDGE

- Do you think a seventeen-year-old should be sentenced to death? Does age matter when such a horrible crime is committed?

- Did the death penalty violate Christopher's Eighth Amendment rights?

- Do you think older teens are prepared to accept responsibility for their behavior, even a lengthy prison sentence or the death penalty?

THE RULING

The ultimate question before the Court was whether age alone was enough to spare someone from the death penalty. The Court analyzed the issue by looking at the nation's attitude about crime and punishment, particularly the use of the death penalty. In order to determine if **capital punishment** was "cruel and unusual" for minors under the Eighth Amendment, the Court first reviewed current state laws to see how society viewed punishment. (Because laws are passed by state representatives, they're assumed to represent the beliefs of people who live in that state.) It also reviewed other Court decisions that placed restrictions on the death penalty for certain groups of the population, as well as foreign laws on executions of minors.

In a five to four decision written by Justice Anthony M. Kennedy, the Court found that historically the law recognized that children and adults have different rights and duties. Most states treat people under eighteen as minors and place certain restrictions on them. For example, minors usually cannot enter into contracts by themselves, vote, get married without parental consent, be jurors, or buy alcohol or cigarettes.

The Court accepted the argument that the average seventeen-year-old isn't prepared to assume the full responsibilities of an adult. The Court considered adult versus juvenile behavior and said that less experience, education, and maturity makes teenagers less able to evaluate the consequences of their conduct. Teenagers are much more likely than adults to be motivated by emotion or peer pressure. It wrote: "The character of a juvenile is not as well formed as that of an adult." Therefore, the Court reasoned, juveniles aren't trusted with the privileges and responsibilities of an adult, and their crimes aren't as morally unacceptable as those of adults.

The Court also found that a "national consensus" had developed against using the death penalty for minors; it was considered "cruel and unusual punishment" and thus was unconstitutional. Additionally, the Court considered the international consensus against executing minors.

The Court concluded that when a juvenile commits a horrifying crime, the state can deprive him or her of basic liberties but cannot extinguish his or her life and potential to attain a mature under-standing of his or her own humanity. "The age of 18 is the point where society draws the line for many purposes between childhood and adulthood. It is, we conclude, the age at which the line for death penalty eligibility ought to rest," wrote the Court.

With the 2005 *Roper v. Simmons* ruling, the United States became the last coun-try in the world to either abolish or disapprove the death penalty for juvenile offenders.

Following the Court's decision, Christopher's sentence was reduced to life imprisonment without the possibility of parole. The justices who disagreed with the majority wrote two **dissents** on the case. Both dissents, written by Justices Antonin Scalia and Sandra Day O'Connor, questioned the "national consensus" against the death penalty for minors—whether it was indeed formed and the relevance of it in considering the case. Scalia also objected to the review of foreign law in the case.

When the U.S. Supreme Court rules that a state law violates the U.S. Constitution, individual states can take action and remove the law from their books—as Missouri may do now that the Court has ruled that their law allowing the juvenile death penalty violates the Constitution—or they can leave it on the books as a void law, which is unenforceable.

RELATED CASES

Courts are constantly being pressed to decide what types of punishment are fair, reasonable, and acceptable in the eyes of society. The justices who consider these cases can't rely solely on their per-sonal values; they must also carefully review the Constitution and the beliefs of the citizens of this country in reaching a conclusion. And at no time will their decisions satisfy everyone.

- **Should people who are severely mentally challenged be eligible for the death penalty?**

In 1996, Daryl Renard Atkins and Williams Jones abducted and robbed Eric Nesbitt. They took him to an isolated area where he was then murdered. Atkins was found guilty of all three crimes and was sentenced to death. His attorney argued, and a psychologist confirmed, that Atkins was slightly mentally retarded. His sentence was appealed and his attorneys argued that the death penalty was "excessive" for someone with his IQ.

The U.S. Supreme Court agreed to review the issue of executing people who are mentally retarded. The Court had last looked at the issue in a 1989 case *(Penry v. Lynaugh)* and at the time stated that mental disabilities are a factor that may well lessen a person's responsibilities for a capital crime, but mental retardation did not automatically rule out capital punishment. In 2002, however, the Court ruled that the national consensus had changed and the death penalty was now considered "cruel and unusual punishment" for people who are mentally retarded. Mentally retarded criminals cannot be held to the same level of responsibility as other adults.

Atkins v. Virginia (2002)

- **What about sentencing a minor to life in prison without the possibility of parole? Is this cruel and unusual punishment?**

Sixteen-year-old Stephen Launsburry and a friend wanted to leave town and flagged down a car driven by a pregnant woman. While attempting to steal the woman's car, Stephen shot and killed her. He was sentenced to life without the possibility of parole. The Michigan Court of Appeals upheld the sentence, stating it "does not constitute cruel and unusual punishment."

People v. Launsburry (1996)

- **What if the juvenile is only thirteen? Is life without the possibility of parole acceptable then?**

For a year, thirteen-year-old Khamsone Naovarath had been molested by his thirty-eight-year-old neighbor, David Foote, who was confined to a wheelchair. On January 1, 1987, Khamsone forced his way into David's house and brutally tortured him, until finally stabbing him several times and strangling him with an electrical cord. Khamsone confessed to the murder, saying he didn't know why he did it.

He was sentenced to life in prison without the possibility of parole. On appeal, the Nevada Supreme Court reduced the sentence to life *with* a possibility of parole. It said: "[A] flicker of light should be kept alive in the hope that he may some time in the future be rehabilitated and become an acceptable member of society."
Naovarath v. State (1989)

• What if parole isn't possible for at least thirty years? Is this cruel and unusual, no matter what the crime?

In November 1994, fifteen-year-old Eric Mitchell robbed a convenience store in Minnesota with seventeen-year-old Harley Hildenbrand, who acted as a lookout. Eric went into the store and confronted the nineteen-year-old clerk, Mickey Wilfert. Although the security cameras showed no resistance by Mickey, Eric shot him in the face. Eric was tried as an adult, and a jury convicted him of intentional first-degree murder. He was sentenced to the mandatory adult sentence—life imprisonment with no possibility of parole for a minimum of thirty years. He and his lawyer appealed, arguing that his sentence was cruel and unusual punishment based on his age. The Minnesota Supreme Court upheld the sentence, finding no violation of Eric's rights or that the sentence was cruel and unusual. It said: "Mitchell committed one of the most heinous crimes, murder in the first degree. . . . [W]e cannot say that his punishment was out of proportion to his crime."
State v. Eric Mitchell (1998)

• Do the circumstances of a case affect whether a sentence is appropriate?

In August 1993, Jason Pilcher and Brandy Wiley (both fifteen) ran away together. They stole a car and a loaded .38 revolver. Jason was driving when he lost control of the car and crashed into a ditch. They walked to a nearby house and asked to use the phone. Phyllis Albritton's eleven-year-old son, Justin, brought them a cordless phone. His thirteen-year-old sister, Amanda, brought them each a glass of water. Without provocation, Jason pulled the gun out and killed Mrs. Albritton. He chased Justin to his room and killed him. Amanda ran out the back door and was shot at, but not hit. Jason was convicted in Louisiana of two counts of murder. He received two life sentences, to be served one after the other. He appealed and the court ruled that the sentences, without the opportunity of parole, **probation,** or suspension, were not excessive or illegal under the circumstances of this case.

State v. Pilcher (1995)

GET ON THE CASE

- Do you think a teenager should be locked up for the rest of his or her life for committing a murder? Should the circumstances of the incident be considered and the jury or court given the ability to decide the length of sentence? How much consideration should be given to the victim and the victim's family?

- What do you think about the evolving national consensus on topics such as the death penalty? Do you agree that the Constitution needs to be interpreted using today's beliefs and standards?

- Do you think the death sentence is cruel and unusual punishment for anyone—adults and minors alike? Or do you agree it's an appropriate sentence for some crimes? What about the different forms of execution—lethal injection, electrocution, gas chamber, hanging, or firing squad? Some controversy exists about whether one form is more humane than another, and some forms are rarely used anymore. What do you think? Are some forms of execution more acceptable than others? Why or why not?

- With your classmates or family, hold a mock debate on the death penalty. Assign or choose sides of the issue, and then research the arguments and start the debate.

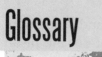
Glossary

Accomplice. A person who voluntarily helps someone commit, or attempt to commit, a crime.

Age of majority. In most states, eighteen is recognized as the age of adulthood, entitling you to make your own decisions and manage your personal affairs.

Appeal. A right that is sometimes available to the losing party of a case, depending on the type of case. It allows you to ask a higher court (called an *appellate court*) to review a decision made by a lower court. The appellate court decides the case by reviewing a transcript of what took place in the lower court. The court doesn't consider new evidence; there are no witnesses called to testify; and there is no jury. The attorneys involved make their arguments to the court in writing (called briefs), and they may be allowed to present oral arguments, if the court thinks it would be useful in deciding the issues. The appellate court has the power to reverse the decision of the lower court and send the case back for a new trial, affirm the trial court's decision, or modify the decision.

Bill of Rights. The first ten amendments to the United States Constitution.

Brief. A concise written statement about a case, with arguments about issues raised by the lawyers. Briefs are read by the appellate court and help in making decisions about these issues.

Capacity to sue. The ability of a person to come into court under his or her own name. This right is usually limited to adults and emancipated minors.

Capital crime. Crime that may be punishable by death.

Capital punishment. The death penalty.

Censorship. The act of limiting access to material found objectionable; for example, books, movies, and music with explicit sexual content, violence, or profanity. Schools also have the right to limit what is contained in a student publication or play.

Child endangerment. This term is defined by each state. Sometimes it's considered the same thing as child abuse, and usually involves the intentional harm of a child. The Iowa definition of endangerment, for example, is the intentional use of physical force that results in physical injury.

Child protection laws. Laws in every state that provide for the protection of minors from abuse and neglect.

Civil commitment laws. The right to hospitalize people who are a danger to themselves or others against their will—without being charged with a crime.

Civil detention. Detaining someone to protect him or her from possibly harming himself or herself, or others.

Concurring opinion. A separate opinion written by a justice of an appellate court that agrees with the majority decision.

Confrontation. Questioning a witness in court. Every person charged with a crime has the right to cross-examine people who are accusing or testifying against him or her in court.

Contempt of court. Anything that interferes with the work of the court, including failing to follow a judge's order. The penalty may be a fine or jail time.

Corporal punishment. Physical discipline such as swats, paddling, and spanking.

Criminal detention. Detaining a minor who has been charged with a crime in a juvenile facility. State laws dictate the type and length of confinement.

Cross-examination. Questioning a witness in court. Every person charged with a crime has the right to face people who are accusing or testifying against him or her in court.

Delinquent. A minor who violates a criminal law. If found guilty, he or she is called a juvenile delinquent.

Detention. Temporary confinement of a minor in a locked facility. Although it isn't considered jail, the juvenile can't leave. This may be a consequence of an action committed by the minor or for the safety of the minor or the community between hearings. A person with a mental illness may also be held (detained) for certain periods of time if authorities believe the person is a danger to self or others.

Discrimination. The act of treating an individual or a group differently than others because of race, gender, religion, nationality, or disability. Not all discrimination is illegal. Teenagers have age restrictions regarding employment, curfew, alcohol, and driving, all of which is legal.

Dissenting opinion. An opinion written by a justice of an appellate court that explains why the justice disagrees with the majority decision. Other justices may also join the dissenting opinion.

Diversion. A method of handling thousands of low misdemeanor offenses, usually for first-time offenders. With diversion, no formal charges are filed and no one goes to court. Instead, the offender admits the offense, usually to a probation officer or an administrative person, and is given a consequence such as community service hours and/or restitution and the case is closed. In this way, the matter is diverted away from the judicial system

Due process. Also called *due process of law,* this is your right to enforce and protect your basic rights to life, liberty, and property. It means that you have the right to be notified of any action against you and the right to be heard and confront the opposing side. Essentially, it's the right to fair treatment.

Emancipation. The process of becoming legally free from your parents or guardian. This may be the result of a court order, an act on your part (marriage, enlistment in the armed services), or other circumstances your state's law allows. If you're emancipated, your parents lose their authority over you and are no longer responsible for you.

Equal protection. The principle that everyone in the same group or classification should be treated the same. A person can't be singled out of a group and treated differently.

Establishment Clause. A part of the First Amendment. It means that the government may not promote or affiliate itself with any religious teaching or organization. Government may not advance or inhibit religion, or aid, foster, or promote one religion over another. Federal and state governments are to be neutral in all religious matters.

Extended jurisdiction law. Law that gives the juvenile court authorization to impose a sentence that goes beyond the legal age of eighteen or twenty-one, depending on the state. This is referred to as a blended sentence because it crosses over from one jurisdiction (juvenile) to another (adult) upon reaching a designated age.

Felony. A classification of the criminal laws that carries the strictest penalties, usually a minimum of one year in jail. A felony is more serious than a misdemeanor or petty offense.

Guardian. An individual with the legal power and duty to take care of another person, including his or her property and financial affairs. The court may appoint a guardian for a minor if necessary, and sometimes the minor may select a guardian or object to the one being considered. A guardian may also be selected by your parents and named in their will.

Guardian ad litem. Latin for "guardian at law," this is a person the court appoints to represent a minor in a specific case. Once the case is over, the guardian is dismissed. This person's job is to present to the court what he or she thinks is in the minor's best interest, and that may not be what the minor is asking for. A lawyer, on the other hand, is responsible for presenting his or her client's position in a case. That is why a minor may have both a lawyer and a guardian ad litem.

Judicial bypass procedure. A procedure used when a minor seeks an abortion and doesn't want to tell her parents, for whatever reason. In this situation, the minor may show the court she is mature enough and well enough informed to make a decision, in consultation with her doctor, and independent of her parents' wishes. If not mature enough, she may show the abortion is in her best interests.

Jurisdiction. The legal right of a judge and a court to exercise its authority—the power to hear and determine a case. Specific rules exist regarding jurisdiction. Without it, a court is powerless to act. Under some circumstances, a juvenile court may waive its jurisdiction over you and ask an adult court to consider your case.

Juvenile delinquent. A minor who has broken the law and has either admitted the offense or been found guilty by a court.

Minor. Someone who's not yet legally an adult.

Miranda rights. These are the rights that suspects are read when in police custody. You have the right to remain silent; a right to a lawyer before you talk to the police; if you can't afford to hire a lawyer yourself, one will be appointed to you; and the right to have your parents with you during questioning. If, after you've been told of these rights, you choose to talk to the police, whatever you say may be used against you later on.

Misdemeanor. A criminal offense less serious than a *felony*, with a jail sentence of one year or less.

Negligence. Doing something a reasonable and careful person wouldn't do, or failing to do something a reasonable and careful person would do under similar circumstances. As a result of the person's act or omission, an injury occurs.

Petition. Asking the court, in writing, to take a specific action regarding a person or company.

Petty offense. A crime with a maximum penalty of (usually) a few months in jail or a fine. No prison time is given, and the fines are often set by law up to several hundred dollars.

Probation. A program in which you're supervised by the court or probation department for a period of time. Special terms of probation may include time in detention, community service hours, counseling, a fine, or restitution.

Probation officer. An officer of the court assigned to a minor or an adult placed on probation. This person arranges for appropriate services to assist with rehabilitation, provides supervision and guidance, and reports results to the court.

Restitution. The act of restoring a victim to the position the victim was in before suffering property damages or loss or personal injury. A minor placed on probation may be required to pay back the victim for any loss the minor caused.

Search and seizure. The ability of a person in a position of authority (police or schoolteacher) to search you or your property (room, car, locker) and take anything unlawful or not legally in your possession.

Sexual harassment. Any unwelcome sexual advances, request for sexual favors, or other verbal or physical contact of a sexual nature—to be unlawful, it must be so offensive and severe that the conduct affects or disrupts the victim's education or ability to do his or her job.

Social file. A file separate from the court's legal file. It contains a person's social history, previous evaluations, and probation officer's reports.

Statutory rape. Unlawful sexual relations with a person under the age of consent, which may be sixteen, seventeen, or eighteen, depending on your state. It's a crime even if the underage person consents.

Subpoena. A formal written document that commands an individual to appear in court to testify as a witness. Failure to appear will result in a penalty.

Transfer. In juvenile law, this is the process by which a minor is charged with a crime and tried in adult court rather than juvenile court. Due to the seriousness of the charge and the juvenile's history, he or she may be treated as an adult, making the juvenile eligible for adult consequences including life imprisonment.

Waive. To voluntarily give up or transfer a right. For example, a person can waive his or her right to a trial by jury; juvenile courts can waive their jurisdiction of a trial to an adult court.

Warrant. A written order from a court directing law enforcement to either arrest an individual or search a specific place for evidence of a crime.

Zone and expectation of privacy. The area that a reasonable person would expect to be protected from the intrusion of others—an area outside of public view or where one has taken precautions to preserve his or her privacy.

Bibliography

Rachel Kingsley v. Gregory Kingsley (1993)

A Kind and Just Parent: The Children of Juvenile Court by William Ayers (Boston: Beacon Press, 1997).

No Matter How Loud I Shout: A Year in the Life of Juvenile Court by Edward Humes (New York: Simon & Schuster, 1996).

"The Most Valuable Clients: Attorneys Must Deal with Special Issues When Kids Come into Contact with the Courts" by Margaret Graham Tebo, 89 *American Bar Association Journal* 48 (April 2003).

Taming the Lawyers: What to Expect in a Lawsuit and How to Make Sure Your Attorney Gets Results by Kenneth Menendez (Morton, PA: Silver Lake Publishing, 1996).

Meyer v. Nebraska (1923)

Abandoned in the Wasteland: Children, Television and the First Amendment by Newton N. Minow, Craig L. Lamay (New York: Hill and Wang, 1995).

"Criminal and Civil Parental Liability Statutes: Would They Have Saved the Fifteen Who Died at Columbine?" by Eric Paul Ebenstein, 7 *Cardozo Women's Law Journal* 1 (2000).

"Holding Parents Criminally Responsible for the Delinquent Acts of Their Children: Reasoned Response or 'Knee-Jerk Reaction'?" by Christine T. Greenwood, 23 *Journal of Contemporary Law* 401 (1997).

"Killer Party: Proposing Civil Liability for Social Hosts Who Serve Alcohol to Minors" by Matthew C. Houchens, 30 *John Marshall Law Review* 245 (1996).

Gebser v. Lago Vista Independent School District (1998)

"A Rose by Any Other Name . . . The Gender Basis of Same-Sex Sexual Harassment" by Robert Brookins, 46 *Drake Law Review* 441 (1998).

Sexual Harassment: High School Girls Speak Out by June Larkin (Toronto: Second Story Press, 1994).

Sexual Harassment: What Teens Should Know (Issues in Focus) by Carol Rust Nash (Springfield, NJ: Enslow Publishers Inc., 1996).

Sexual Harassment and Teens: A Program for Positive Change by Susan Strauss with Pamela Espeland (Minneapolis: Free Spirit Publishing, 1992).

Sexual Harassment on Campus: A Guide for Administrators, Faculty, and Students by Bernice R. Sandler, Robert J. Shoop, and Carolyn S. Bratt (Needham Heights, MA: Allyn & Bacon, 1996).

Beth Ann Faragher v. City of Boca Raton (1998)

Everything You Need to Know About Sexual Harassment (Need to Know Library) by Elizabeth Bouchard (New York: Rosen Publishing Company, 1997).

Rights and Respect: What You Need to Know About Gender Bias and Sexual Harassment by Kathyln Gay (Brookfield, CT: Millbrook Press, 1995).

Sexual Harassment: A Practical Guide to the Law, Your Rights, and Your Options for Taking Action by Tracy O'Shea and Jane Lalonde (New York: St. Martin's Griffin, 1998).

Sexual Harassment and Teens: A Program for Positive Change by Susan Strauss with Pamela Espeland (Minneapolis: Free Spirit Publishing, 1992).

You Want Me to Do What? When, Where and How to Draw the Line at Work by Nan DeMars (New York: Fireside, 1998).

Vernonia School District v. Jimmy Acton (1995)

Addiction: The High That Brings You Down by Miriam Smith McLaughlin (Springfield, NJ: Enslow Publishers Inc., 1997).

"The Constitution Expelled: What Remains of Students' Fourth Amendment Rights?" by Darrell Jackson, 28 *Arizona State University Law Journal* 673 (1996).

Drugs and Sports by Rodney G. Peck (New York: Rosen Publishing Group, 1998).

"From the Classroom to the Courtroom: Reassessing Fourth Amendment Standards in Public School Searches Involving Law Enforcement Authorities" by Michael Pinard, 45 *Arizona Law Review* 1067 (Winter 2003).

"High School Students Lose Their Rights When They Don Their Uniforms" by Jonathan M. Ettman, 13 *New York Law School Journal of Human Rights* 625 (1997).

"Schools Can Test Students in Extracurricular Activities for Drug Use," *Supreme Court Debates,* Vol. 5 No. 6 (Sept. 2002).

New Jersey v. T. L. O. (1985)

"Minors and the Fourth Amendment: How Juvenile Status Should Invoke Different Standards for Searches and Seizures on the Streets" by Lourdes M. Rosado, 71 *New York Law Review* 762 (1996).

New Jersey v. T. L. O., Drug Searches in Schools by Deborah A. Persico (Springfield, NJ: Enslow Publishers Inc., 1998).

The Right to Privacy by Ellen Alderman and Caroline Kennedy (New York: Knopf Publishers, 1995).

"Strip Searches of Students: What Johnny Really Learned at School and How Local School Boards Can Help Solve the Problem" by Scott A. Gartner, 70 *Southern California Law Review* 921 (March 1997).

"Student Designed Home Web Pages: Does Title IX or the First Amendment Apply?" by Susan H. Kosse, 43 *Arizona Law Review* 905 (Winter 2001).

Tariq A-R Y v. Maryland (1998)

"And a Small Child Shall Lead Them: The Validity of Children's Consent to Warrantless Searches of the Family Home" by Matt McCaughey, 34 *University of Louisville Journal of Family Law* 747 (Summer 1995–1996).

"Changing with the Times: Why Rampant School Violence Warrants Legalization of Parental Wiretapping to Monitor Children's Activities" by Alison S. Aaronson, 9 *Journal of Law and Policy* 785 (2001).

Mind Your Own Business: The Battle for Personal Privacy by Gini Graham Scott (New York: Insight Books, 1995).

"Minors and the Fourth Amendment: How Juvenile Status Should Invoke Different Standards for Searches and Seizures on the Streets" by Lourdes M. Rosado, 71 *New York University Law Review* 762 (1996).

Kent v. United States (1966)

"Blended Sentences: A Good Idea for Juvenile Sex Offenders?" by Kristin L. Caballero, 19 *St. John's Journal of Legal Commentary* 379 (Winter 2005).

"Dennis the Menace or Billy the Kid: An Analysis of the Role of Transfer to Criminal Court in Juvenile Justice" by Eric K. Klein, 35 *American Criminal Law Review* 371 (Winter 1998).

"49 Black Faces, Brown Faces . . . Why Are We Different Than White Faces? An Analytical Comparison of the Rate of Certification of Minority & Non-Minority Juvenile Offenders" by Keisha L. David, 2 *Scholar: St. Mary's Law Review on Minority Issues* 49 (2000).

"Justice or Vengeance: How Young is Too Young for a Child to Be Tried and Punished as an Adult?" by Jarod K. Hofacket, 34 *Texas Tech Law Review* 159 (2002).

"Juvenile Delinquency in the Twenty-First Century: Is Blended Sentencing the Middle-Road Solution for Violent Kids?" by Christine Sullivan, 21 *Northern Illinois University Law Review* 483 (2001).

"Tenuous Borders: Girls Transferred to Adult Court" by Emily Gaarder and Joanne Belknap, 40 *Criminology* 481 (August 2002).

Bellotti v. Baird (1979)

The Abortion Battle: Looking at Both Sides by Felicia Lowenstein (Springfield, NJ: Enslow Publishers Inc., 1996).

Dear Diary, I'm Pregnant: Teenagers Talk About Their Pregnancy by Annrenée Englander (Toronto: Annick Press, 1997).

Griswold v. Connecticut: Contraception and the Right of Privacy by Susan C. Wawrose (Danbury, CT: Franklin Watts, 1996).

"Partial-Birth Abortion: Crime or Protected Right?" by Melissa DeRosa, 16 *St. John's Journal of Legal Commentary* 199 (2002).

"Sex Education and Condom Distribution: John, Susan, Parents, and Schools" by Jeffrey F. Caruso, *Notre Dame Journal of Law, Ethics and Public Policy*, Vol. 10, No. 2 (1996).

Sex Smart: 501 Reasons to Hold Off on Sex by Susan Browning Pogany (Minneapolis: Fairview Press, 1998).

Planned Parenthood Locator Service
1-800-230-7526
www.plannedparenthood.org
Planned Parenthood believes in the fundamental right of each individual, throughout the world, to manage his or her fertility, regardless of the individual's income, marital status, race, ethnicity, sexual orientation, age, national origin, or residence. Contact them to find a clinic in your area.

Tinker v. Des Moines Independent School District (1969)

"At Daggers Dawn: The Confederate Flag and the School Classroom—A Case Study of a Broken First Amendment Formula" by James M. Dedman, 53 *Baylor Law Review* 877 (Fall 2001).

"The Right to Write? Free Expression Rights of Pennsylvania's Creative Students After Columbine" by Barbara J. Brunner, 107 *Dickinson Law Review* 891 (2003).

The Struggle for Student Rights: Tinker v. Des Moines and the 1960s by John W. Johnson (Lawrence, KS: University Press of Kansas, 1997).

Tinker v. Des Moines: Student Protest by Leah Farish (Springfield, NJ: Enslow Publishers Inc., 1997).

Olff v. East Side Union High School District (1972)

Ferrell v. Dallas Ind. School District—Hairstyles in Schools by Karen L. Trespacz (Springfield, NJ: Enslow Publishers Inc., 1998).

"No Shoes, No Shirt, No Education: Dress Codes and Freedom of Expression Behind the Postmodern Schoolhouse Gates" by Alison G. Myhra, *Seton Hall Constitutional Law Journal* 337 (Spring 1999).

"Public School Dress Codes: The Constitutional Debate" by Amy Mitchell Wilson, 1998 *BYU Education and Law Journal* 147 (Spring 1998), pages 147–172.

"Undressing the First Amendment in Public Schools: Do Uniform Dress Codes Violate a Student's First Amendment Rights?" by Alison M. Barbarosh, 28 *Loyola University (Los Angeles) Law Review* 1415 (1995).

Education Week
www.edweek.org
Education Week is for people interested in education reform, schools, and the policies that guide them.

Hazelwood School District v. Kuhlmeier (1988)

Hazelwood v. Kuhlmeier—Censorship in School Newspapers by Sarah Betsy Fuller (Springfield, NJ: Enslow Publishers Inc., 1998).

"Kids Surfing the Net at School: What Are the Legal Issues?" by Sally Rutherford, 24 *Rutgers Computer & Technology Law Journal* 417 (1998).

"Only the News That's Fit to Print: The Effect of Hazelwood on the First Amendment Viewpoint-Neutrality Requirement in Public Schools" by Janna J. Annest, 77 *Washington Law Review* 1227 (Oct. 2002).

"Viewpoint Discrimination" by Marjorie Heins, 24 *Hastings Constitutional Law Quarterly* 99 (1996).

Freedom Forum
www.freedomforum.org
The Freedom Forum is a nonpartisan, international foundation dedicated to free press, free speech, and free spirit for all people. The foundation pursues its priorities through conferences, educational activities, publishing, broadcasting, online services, fellowships, partnerships, training, research, and other programs.

Student Press Law Center
(703) 807-1904
www.splc.org
Since 1974, the Student Press Law Center has been the nation's only legal assistance agency devoted exclusively to educating high school and college journalists about the rights and responsibilities embodied in the First Amendment and supporting the student news media in their struggle to cover important issues free from censorship.

Lee v. Weisman (1992)

"Can 'Moment of Silence' Statutes Survive?" by Michael A. Umayam, 50 *Catholic University Law Review* 869 (Spring 2001).

The First Amendment: Freedom of Speech, Religion, and the Press by Leah Farish (Springfield, NJ: Enslow Publishers Inc., 1998).

Religious Schools v. Children's Rights by James G. Dwyer (Ithaca, NY: Cornell University Press, 1998).

School Prayer: A History of the Debate by Tricia Andryszewski (Springfield, NJ: Enslow Publishers Inc., 1997).

Ingraham v. Wright (1977)

"Corporal Punishment in Public Schools: The Legal and Political Battle Continues" by John Dayton, 89 *Education Law Reporter* 729 (1994).

"Gangs, Schools and Stereotypes" by Linda S. Beres and Thomas D. Griffith, 37 *Loyola Law Review* 935 (Spring 2004).

"'Time-Out' for Student Threats? Imposing a Duty to Protect on School Officials" by Melissa L. Gilbert, 49 *UCLA Law Review* 917 (Feb. 2002).

Joshua DeShaney v. Winnebago County Social Services (1989)

"Banning Child Corporal Punishment" by Deana Pollard, 77 *Tulane Law Review* 575 (Feb. 2003).

"The Dynamics Between Animal Abuse, Domestic Violence and Child Abuse: How Pets Can Help Abused Children" by Allie Phillips, 39 *Prosecutor* 22 (Sept/Oct. 2004).

"Parricide: States Are Beginning to Recognize that Abused Children Who Kill Their Parents Should Be Afforded the Right to Assert a Claim of Self-Defense" by Merrilee R. Goodwin, 25 *Southwestern University Law Review* 429 (1996).

"Spanking and Other Corporal Punishment of Children by Parents: Overvaluing Pain, Undervaluing Children" by David Orentlicher, 35 *Houston Law Review* 147 (1998).

"Spare the Rod, Embrace Our Humanity: Toward a New Legal Regime Prohibiting Corporal Punishment of Children" by Susan H. Bitensky, 31 *University of Michigan Journal of Law Reform* 289 (1998).

"When Is Parental Discipline Child Abuse? The Vagueness of Child Abuse Laws" by Scott A. Davidson, 34 *Journal of Family Law* 403 (1996).

Parham v. J. R. (1979)

"Competency to Stand Trial in Preadjudicated and Petitioned Juvenile Defendants" by Dana Royce Baerger, Eugene F. Griffin, John S. Lyons, and Ron Simmons, 31 *Journal of the American Academy of Psychiatry and the Law* 314 (2003).

Fighting Invisible Tigers: A Stress Management Guide for Teens by Earl Hipp (Minneapolis: Free Spirit Publishing, 1995).

Talk with Teens About Self and Stress: 50 Guided Discussions for School and Counseling Groups by Jean Sunde Peterson and Pamela Espeland (Minneapolis: Free Spirit Publishing, 1993).

"Those Crazy Kids: Providing the Insanity Defense in Juvenile Courts" by Emily S. Pollack, 85 *Minnesota Law Review* 2041 (June 2001).

When Nothing Matters Anymore: A Survival Guide for Depressed Teens by Bev Cobain (Minneapolis: Free Spirit Publishing, 1998).

Parkerson v. Brooks (1995)

"The Best Interests of All Children: An Examination of Grandparent Visitation Rights Regarding Children Born Out of Wedlock" by Nicole Miller, 42 *New York Law Review* 179 (Summer 1997).

"Breaking Up a Family or Putting It Back Together Again" by Carolyn Wilkes Kaas, 37 *William and Mary Law Review* 1045 (1996).

"Can My Daddy Hug Me? Deciding Whether Visiting Dad in a Prison Facility Is in the Best Interests of the Child" by Rachel Sims, 66 *Brooklyn Law Review* 933 (2000–2001).

My Parents Are Getting Divorced: A Handbook for Kids (Chicago: American Bar Association Family Advocate, 1996). Call 1-800-285-2221 to order a copy of this guide.

"Now I Lay Me Down to Sleep: A Look at Overnight Visitation Rights Available to Incarcerated Mothers" by Rachel D. Costa, 29 *New England Journal on Criminal and Civil Confinement* 67 (Winter 2003).

"A Quest for Sibling Visitation: Daniel Weber's Story" by Christine D. Markel, 18 *Whittier Law Review* 863 (1997).

"Sibling Rights to Visitation: A Relationship Too Valuable to Be Denied" by Joel V. Williams, 27 *University of Toledo Law Review* 259 (Fall 1995).

In re Gault (1967)

"Are Police Free to Disregard Miranda?" by Steven D. Clymer, 112 *Yale Law Journal* 447 (Dec. 2002).

"Good Kids, Bad Kids: A Revelation About the Due Process Rights of Children" by Cecilia M. Espenoza, 23 *Hastings Constitutional Law Quarterly* 407 (Winter 1996).

"I Didn't Do It, I Was Forced to Say That I Did: The Problem of Coerced Juvenile Confessions" by Nashiba F. Boyd, 47 *Howard Law Journal* 395 (Winter 2004).

In re Gault (1967): Juvenile Justice by Susan Dudley Gold (New York: Twenty-First Century Books, 1995).

"Miranda in a Juvenile Setting: A Child's Right to Silence" by Larry E. Holtz, 78 *Journal of Criminal Law & Criminology* 534 (1987).

Josh Davis v. Alaska (1974)

"Disclosing the Identities of Juvenile Felons: Introducing Accountability to Juvenile Justice" by Arthur R. Blum, 27 *Loyola University Chicago Law Journal* 349 (Winter 1996).

"A Mere Youthful Indiscretion? Reexamining the Policy of Expunging Juvenile Delinquency Records" by T. Markus Funk, 29 *University of Michigan Journal of Law Ref.* 885 (1996)

"Newspaper Access to Juvenile Court Records" by Linda A. Szymanski, 34 *Juvenile and Family Law Digest*, No. 1 (Jan. 2002).

"Privacy v. Public Access to Juvenile Court Proceedings: Do Closed Hearings Protect the Child or the System?" by Jan L. Trasen, 15 *Boston College Third World Law Journal* 359 (1995).

McKeiver v. Pennsylvania (1971)

The Jury: Disorder in the Court by Stephen J. Adler (New York: Main Street Books, 1995).

Jury Trials in the Classroom by Betty M. See and Diane Elizabeth See (Englewood, CO: Teacher Ideas Press, 1998).

"Reflections on Judges, Juries and Justice: Ensuring the Fairness of Juvenile Delinquency Trials" by Guggenhein and Hertz, 33 *Wake Forest Law Review* 553 (1998).

"The Right to a Public Jury Trial: A Need for Today's Juvenile Court" by Joseph B. Sanborn, 76 *Judicature* 230 (1993).

Roper v. Simmons (2005)

"Critique of the Juvenile Death Penalty in the United States: A Global Perspective" by Lori Edwards, 42 *Duquesne Law Review* 317 (Winter 2004).

Dead Man Walking (1995). This movie takes a powerful, but balanced, look at capital punishment, starring Susan Sarandon and Sean Penn.

"The Efficacy of Harsh Punishment for Teenage Violence" by Victor L. Streib, 31 *Valparaiso University Law Review* 427 (1997).

"Too Young to Die—Juveniles and the Death Penalty—A Better Alternative to Killing Our Children: Youth Empowerment" by Sherri Jackson, 22 *New England Journal of Criminal & Civil Confinement* (1996).

"When Will It Stop? The Use of the Death Penalty for Non-Homicide Crimes" by Jeffrey C. Matura, 24 *Journal of Legislation* 249 (1998).

Index

About the Author

Thomas A. Jacobs, J.D., attended Loyola University at Los Angeles and Arizona State University College of Law. He served as an Arizona Assistant Attorney General from 1972 to 1985, handling civil, criminal, and child welfare matters. In 1985, he was appointed to the Maricopa County Superior Court, Juvenile Division, where he presided over delinquency, dependency, severance, and adoption cases. In 2001, he was assigned to Family Court, where he remained until retiring in 2002. A regular speaker and instructor at community functions and educational programs, he also taught for ten years at the Arizona State University School of Social Work. After thirty years in law, he was appointed a part-time judge in 2003, assigned to handle adoptions. Judge Jacobs continues to write about the law for teens, lawyers, and judges.

Other Great Books from Free Spirit

They Broke the Law—You Be the Judge
True Cases of Teen Crime
by Thomas A. Jacobs, J.D.
This book invites teens to preside over a variety of real-life cases, to learn each teen's background, the relevant facts, and the sentencing options available. After deciding on a sentence, they find out what really happened—and where each offender is today. A thought-provoking introduction to the juvenile justice system. For ages 12 & up. *$15.95; 224 pp.; softcover; 6" x 9"*

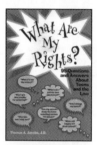

What Are My Rights?
95 Questions and Answers About Teens and the Law
by Thomas A. Jacobs, J.D.
This fascinating book helps teens understand the law, recognize their responsibilities, and appreciate their rights. For ages 12 & up. *$14.95; 208 pp.; softcover; 6" x 9"*

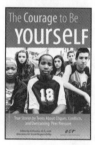

The Courage to Be Yourself
True Stories by Teens About Cliques, Conflicts, and Overcoming Peer Pressure
edited by Al Desetta, M.A., with Educators for Social Responsibility
Jennifer gets harassed because she's overweight. Dwan's family taunts her for not being "black enough." Yen is teased for being Chinese; Jamel for not smoking marijuana. Yet all find the strength to face their conflicts and be themselves. Twenty-six first-person stories. For ages 13 & up. *$13.95, 160 pp.; softcover; 6" x 9"*

Leader's Guide Available
For teachers, social workers, and other adults who work with youth in grades 7–12. *$24.95; 176 pages; softcover; 8½" x 11"*

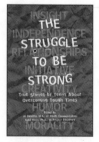

The Struggle to Be Strong
True Stories by Teens About Overcoming Tough Times
edited by Al Desetta, M.A., of Youth Communication, and Sybil Wolin, Ph.D., of Project Resilience
In 30 first-person accounts, teens tell how they overcame major life obstacles. As teens read this book, they'll learn about seven resiliencies—insight, independence, relationships, initiative, creativity, humor, and morality—that everyone needs to overcome tough times. For ages 13 & up. *$14.95; 192 pp.; softcover; illus.; 6" x 9"*

Leader's Guide Available
For teachers, social workers, and other adults who work with youth in grades 7–12. *$21.95; 176 pp.; softcover; 8½" x 11"*

www.freespirit.com